Contents

Chapter 4: Media pluralism and human rights........101
Miklós Haraszti, former OSCE Representative on Freedom of the Media

Chapter 5: Public service media and human rights...133
Boyko Boev, Senior Legal Officer, and Barbora Bukovska, Senior Director for Law and Policy, Article 19

Chapter 6: Social media and human rights...............175

Douwe Korff, Professor of International Law, London Metropolitan University, and Ian Brown, Senior Research Fellow, Oxford Internet Institute, University of Oxford

Foreword: Media freedom in Europe

The media play an enormously important role in the protection of human rights. They expose human rights violations and offer an arena for different voices to be heard in public discourse. Not without reason, the media have been called the Fourth Estate – an essential addition to the powers of the executive, the legislature and the judiciary.

However, the power of the media can also be misused to the extent that the very functioning of democracy is threatened. Some media outlets have been turned into propaganda megaphones for those in power. Others have been used to incite xenophobic hatred and violence against minorities and other vulnerable groups.

The purpose of journalism is not to please those who hold power or to serve as the mouthpiece of governments. Journalists report, investigate and analyse, they inform us about politics, religion, celebrities, the arts, sports, revolutions and wars. They entertain and sometimes annoy us. But most important of all, they are "public watchdogs".

This role is fundamental for democracy. Free, independent and pluralistic media based on freedom of information and expression are a core element of any functioning democracy.

Freedom of the media is also essential for the protection of all other human rights. There are many examples where the misuse of power, corruption, discrimination and even torture have come to light because of the work of investigative journalists. Making the facts known to the public is often the first, essential step in redressing human rights violations and holding those in power accountable.

Public authorities, civil society and the international community, as well as media owners and journalists' organisations, all have important roles to play that reach from law enforcement, education, monitoring and setting universal standards to ethical conduct and self-regulation. The way in which national legislation enshrines media freedom and its practical application by the authorities reveals the state of democracy in the country concerned.

The purpose of this publication is to contribute to a more thorough discussion on various media developments which impact on human rights. Experts were invited to contribute their personal assessments of trends and problems. They were encouraged to raise controversial issues and to provide far-reaching suggestions – also challenging my own views. I would like to thank all eight experts for their high-quality contributions.

The contributions cover:

- protection of journalists from violence;
- ethical journalism;
- access to official documents;
- media pluralism and human rights;
- public service media and human rights;
- social media and human rights.

Together these texts give an indication of the level of protection of media freedom and freedom of expression in Europe today. It is clear that these are topics of paramount importance and demand serious public debate.

In this foreword I summarise some of the most important aspects of each theme. I also make a number of conclusions concerning each theme. The texts and conclusions all revolve around Article 10 of the European Convention on Human Rights (ECHR), which concerns freedom of expression:

1. Everyone has the right to freedom of expression. This right shall include freedom to hold opinions and to receive and impart information and ideas without interference by public authority and regardless of frontiers. This article shall not prevent States from requiring the licensing of broadcasting, television or cinema enterprises.

2. The exercise of these freedoms, since it carries with it duties and responsibilities, may be subject to such formalities, conditions, restrictions or penalties as are prescribed by law and are necessary in a democratic society, in the interests of national security, territorial integrity or public safety, for the prevention of disorder

or crime, for the protection of health or morals, for the protection of the reputation or rights of others, for preventing the disclosure of information received in confidence, or for maintaining the authority and impartiality of the judiciary.

Protection of journalists from violence

In recent years, some of the leading investigative journalists in Europe have been brutally killed: Anna Politkovskaya in Russia, Hrant Dink in Turkey, Georgyi Gongadze in Ukraine and Elmar Huseynov in Azerbaijan.

No effort must be spared to apprehend and bring the perpetrators to justice, as well as those who planned and ordered these murders.

Since 1992 more than 100 journalists have been killed in the Council of Europe region because of their work, including cases of disappearances. Even in more recent years journalists in several countries in Europe have been threatened, sent to prison or murdered for merely doing their job.

Functioning law enforcement and judicial systems are crucial. Both the contract killers and the masterminds behind the crimes must be punished, otherwise they will continue with their cruel business. Impunity creates more impunity. If murders, assaults and threats against journalists prevail, the media cannot be free, information cannot be pluralistic and democracy cannot function.

Threats against one journalist can have the devastating effect of silencing many others. Colleagues of the victims may go on working but fear the danger of reporting and writing about what the public ought to know. Many of them may start to exercise self-censorship.

Another source of concern lies in restrictive laws and other measures to control the media. These tend to have a "chilling effect" on the media directly and a negative impact on society as a whole, across the whole spectrum of human rights. Hungary's new media legislation, for example, raises concerns regarding pre-emptive restraints on press freedom in the form of registration requirements and the imposition of sanctions on the media.

Defamation is still criminalised in several parts of Europe. Laws are in place which make it a criminal offence to speak of or publish facts or opinions that offend a person. Journalists can be put in prison for what they have reported.

This happened for instance in Azerbaijan, where Eynulla Fatullayev (among others) was convicted of defamation and sentenced to imprisonment. The European Court of Human Rights later found that this contravened the ECHR.

The Court noted that "the imposition of a prison sentence for a press offence will not be compatible with journalists' freedom of expression as guaranteed by Article 10 of the ECHR except for exceptional circumstances, notably where other fundamental rights have been seriously impaired, as, for example, in cases of hate speech or incitement to violence".

Reports and comments against the "honour and dignity" of someone should be decriminalised and, if necessary, dealt with in civil law courts, and in a proportionate manner. Prison sentences should no longer be enforced in cases of defamation.

The role of governments in ensuring the safety of journalists is particularly important. It requires strong adherence to human rights principles, determination and perseverance. Governments must demonstrate forcefully that they are prepared to protect the freedom of the media, not only in words, but also through concrete action.

Conclusions

- Political leaders and other opinion builders should strongly condemn violence against journalists. Often aggression against journalists comes from groups and individuals with fundamentalist or extreme nationalist positions. It is important that politicians take a clear stance against such extremism;

- Police and security officials need to effectively protect journalists from danger. Threats have to be taken seriously. The Court has emphasised time and again that the ECHR (Article 2) "enjoins the State not only to refrain from the intentional and unlawful taking of life, but also to take appropriate steps to safeguard the lives of those within its jurisdiction";
- Every case of violence or threats against a journalist must be promptly and professionally investigated. Everyone responsible should be brought to justice;
- Defamation and libel should be decriminalised and unreasonably high fines in civil cases relating to the media should be avoided. Politicians and government officials have to accept a higher degree of public criticism and scrutiny, including from journalists.

Ethical journalism

Sometimes the media unnecessarily and unfairly abuse the privacy and integrity of ordinary people through sheer carelessness or sensationalism and thereby cause considerable damage to them – for no good purpose at all.

As the phone hacking scandal in the United Kingdom showed, competitive pressures may encourage a culture of illegal and unethical activity in the newsroom. This serves no one, least of all shareholders and readers. This is why the media community should be encouraged to develop a system of effective self-regulation based on an agreed code of ethics.

It is obvious that freedom of expression – though an absolutely basic human right – is not without limits. The ECHR makes clear that restrictions may be necessary in the interest of, for instance, national security and public safety. However, the exceptions from the basic rule on everyone's right to freedom of expression must be prescribed by law, serve a legitimate interest and be necessary in a democracy.

The precise definition of such exceptions has been an issue in a number of applications to the Court. Its rulings have clarified that limits to freedom of expression should only be accepted in narrowly defined, exceptional circumstances. This is a logical interpretation of Article 10 of the ECHR as it was originally conceived. One reason for this approach is that censorship, restrictive laws and other measures to control media tend to have a chilling effect on the media community.

The idea of media "self-regulation" springs out of the desire to encourage media structures themselves to develop ethics which would protect individuals or group interests from unacceptable abuse in the media – and thereby demonstrate that state interventions are not necessary. Self-regulation could thus be seen as a solemn promise by quality-conscious journalists and media to correct their mistakes and to make themselves accountable to the public. For this promise to be fulfilled, governments must be restrained in their approach to the media and the work of journalists.

The term "ethical journalism" is highly relevant in this context. Though reporters and editors are not megaphones for particular interests – not even the cause of defending human rights – they can contribute to a better society through genuine professionalism. Ethical journalism is rooted in moral values and has evolved hand in hand with human rights protection in Europe. In essence, ethical journalists serve the public's right to know. They are professional also in the sense that they seek the truth and resist distortions. These are the ethics which should be promoted.

Conclusions

- There should in all member states of the Council of Europe be constitutional support for freedom of expression. Limits to this freedom should be narrowly defined and reflected in law;
- There is a need to encourage a deeper discussion on how to promote ethical journalism, including in relation to Internet-based information;
- The media community should be encouraged to develop a system of effective self-regulation based on an agreed code of ethics and a mechanism to receive and respond to complaints, for instance through an ombudsman or media council;

–   In order to assist efforts by the media to satisfy the public's right to know, governmental and local authorities should respond to queries from journalists. Laws on access to information from public bodies should be enacted, with narrowly defined exceptions for reasons of security, public welfare and individual integrity.

Access to official documents

Pluralist democracies can only thrive through transparency and openness. For "public watchdogs" to be able to play their vital role against the abuse of power – in both public and private enterprises – they must have access to information about what those in power do and decide, and be able to find the documents they need to see. Voters too have the right to know about the decisions taken by their elected politicians and public administrations.

Transparency and open government thus promote fair and equal treatment under the law and efficiency in public administration. The need for such transparency is recognised in principle in several European countries, but is not yet a reality throughout large parts of the continent.

While the authorities collect more and more data on citizens, there is an unfortunate tendency to prevent the public from accessing government information. Journalists who try to obtain copies of official documents from national and local authorities face obstacles and outright refusal in a number of countries. This is why strong legal protection for journalists' sources, particularly for public officials acting as whistle-blowers is also a vital component of transparency.

The Strasbourg Court has already ruled several times on this issue and has consistently made clear that the public has a right to receive information of general interest. The conclusion is that the transparency of public authorities should be regarded as an important element of freedom of information – with a bearing on freedom of expression.

One obvious problem is that the authorities are not always accustomed to dealing with the media in an open manner. This problem has worsened as a consequence of the trend towards further privatisation of services previously organised by local authorities, such as schooling and care for the elderly. Public review of such activities has become more difficult.

There are also instances that demonstrate that decision makers hide behind the supposed need for confidentiality when they feel uncomfortable about possible public reaction to certain facts. This may be one reason why European governments have been reluctant to come clean on the security co-operation with the US during the "war on terror".

There may well be situations where it is justified to keep certain information confidential, for instance to protect national security or the personal integrity of ordinary citizens. To avoid the misuse of such arguments, there is a need for clear regulation on how decisions about confidentiality can be taken and how representatives of the public can challenge such decisions.

There are positive trends which should be recognised. The need for openness is more generally acknowledged nowadays, especially with the growing recognition of the connection between transparency and anti-corruption.

In 2009 the Council of Europe adopted a Convention on Access to Official Documents – the first international legal instrument on access to official documents held by public authorities, including national and local authorities, legislative and judicial bodies as well as natural or legal persons exercising administrative authority.

The constitutions of several countries in Europe do guarantee the fundamental right to information. Some good state practices also exist. In the United Kingdom, for example, the Freedom of Information Act requires public authorities to publish information and sets out procedural requirements to be followed when responding to individual requests.

To facilitate access to government data in the UK, a single online access point has been developed: data.gov.uk. E-government has also become a reality in Estonia and Greece. Citizens can comment on government policies or draft laws by logging into a government Internet portal. In

Serbia and several other countries there is an oversight body – such as an information commissioner – while some other countries entrust a parliamentary ombudsman with the supervision of the right to information. Other countries are yet to create such structures.

The chapter about access to official documents uses Sweden as an example of how open government can be promoted. Citizens' right to access official documents has been constitutionally guaranteed in Sweden for more than 200 years and access rights have traditionally been extended as far as possible in this country. Unfortunately this tendency to maximise transparency has gradually been restricted where citizen access to electronically stored information is concerned.

Conclusions

– Access to government documents based on the principle of transparency has to be ensured. Governments should ratify the 2009 Council of Europe Convention on Access to Official Documents;

– Citizens must be able to find the documents they need to see. To this end there must be strict rules for government agencies on how to register their documents and on obligations to help citizens find what they are looking for;

– Institutions supervising transparency, such as the administrative courts, information commissioners and parliamentary ombudsmen, have important functions in the defence of citizens' right to access information within the public sector;

– Strong legal protection for journalists' sources, particularly for public officials acting as whistle-blowers and assisting the media, is also a vital component of transparency. The right of public officials to inform journalists, on their own initiative and without penalties, should be legally protected.

Media pluralism and human rights

A major threat to media freedom today is the commercialisation and monopoly tendencies we see across Europe. Media pluralism is necessary in order to advance the ends of freedom of speech, and contribute to the development of informed and diverse societies. Pluralism is an effect of freedom of speech, but is also a prerequisite for free speech itself.

However, in some countries, there is no genuine competition: independent television and radio channels are denied licences, critical newspapers have difficulties in buying newsprint or in distributing their papers. Another problem can be that the government buys advertisement space only in the "loyal" media, signalling to business companies to follow their lead, with the consequence that independent media are in reality boycotted. The increase in bureaucratic harassment and administrative discrimination is also of concern.

Concentration of media ownership is yet another problem. If the mass media are dominated by a few companies, the risk for media bias and interference with editorial independence increases. In Italy, for example, the former prime minister is the biggest shareholder of by far the largest private television company (through Fininvest, which owns nearly 39% of the shares of Mediaset). Its *"Canale 5"* is one of the two most-watched television channels in the country.

Ownership transparency is a key administrative tool for breaking up monopolies. If it is known who are the ultimate owners of the broadcasting firms, it is of course possible to break up monopolies and regain trust in media freedom.

Pluralism of the media means a structure that is comprised of competing, diversified, independent media outlets, covering all corners of society, and conveying a great variety of information and opinion. Technological development has created new possibilities for the emergence of such a media landscape. In the digital and Internet era, with the number of accessible channels and audiovisual platforms quickly multiplying, the urgency for detailed regulation – aimed at avoiding political domination – will fade. However, this development may be seen by power holders as justification for more regulatory intrusion.

Conclusions

–   There is a need for a concrete policy to ensure plurality of media, including among the traditional media;

- Monopoly tendencies need to be systematically countered;
- There must be transparency of media ownership;
- The independence of regulators is fundamental and should be secured.

Public service media and human rights

Public service media have an essential role as a counterbalance to the business-driven entertainment media and media empires. Being independent and non-reliant on advertisers they should also encourage good, investigative journalism and knowledge-based content.

The concept of public service media is not often linked to human rights, but it can indeed play a vital role in assuring media freedom and diversity. Well-functioning public service media can be decisive in the protection of human rights, particularly freedom of expression, and provide room for all voices in society, not least minorities, children and other groups which tend to be marginalised.

Where there are strong public service media I can see that there is often high-quality, ethical journalism. Yet, in many countries in Europe, the utility of public service media is being called into question, and sometimes campaigns are conducted against them.

In the Internet age, we have a broader and more interactive media landscape and it has become logical to discuss the broader concept of public service media rather than just public service broadcasting. The former is much more than radio and TV; it has a wider scope in terms of services and it includes both traditional media and new media.

There are two major threats to media pluralism and diversity across Europe today. One is the attempt by state authorities to dominate the media market. The other is commercialisation and tendencies towards monopoly.

It has been argued that there is no objective truth, so impartial reporting is an illusion. The argument that all media presentations will always be more or less biased is one that can be used against state media but not against true public service media. The point is whether there is a genuine ambition to seek impartiality and whether there are safeguards to this end.

Here the link to human rights is particularly relevant. With a rights-based approach for the further development of public service media – encompassing principles of human rights, accountability, participation, non-discrimination and empowerment – their credibility will be strengthened and thereby their potential to act in the interest of the public.

Conclusions

– The independence and impartiality of public service media should be protected. They should neither be commercial nor state-owned, and must be free from political interference and pressure from commercial forces;

– Public service media should include interests for which there are no large markets. They should aim at providing impartial news across the nation, give room to minority interests and remain clear of undue market influence;

– There is a need for studies and exchanges on how public service media actually function across Europe today and to what extent they incorporate human rights principles. This discussion must include the steps necessary to ensure that the potential of Internet-based social media will be fully exploited in the service of the public;

– There is a need to discuss the promotion of genuinely independent and useful public service media, including their mandate, organisation and funding, and accountability.

Social media and human rights

In 2009 the Council of Europe Conference of Ministers responsible for Media and New Communication Services adopted the Reykjavik Declaration. It clarifies that, even if access to the Internet is not a human right per se, in the modern world all Council of Europe member states have a duty to provide or at least permit it.

Social media come with potential problems, as well as gains. This new phenomenon presents us with a range of fresh challenges. One important issue is how to ensure that Internet regulations do not strangle freedom of expression.

"Blocking", for example, is nowadays frequently used to prevent specific content from reaching a final user. However, the indications are that this method is not efficient in preventing, for example, human rights violations on the Internet. Furthermore, who should decide what is to be blocked, and what processes and remedies should this be subject to?

The 2011 Report of the UN Special Rapporteur on Freedom of Opinion and Expression is a strong statement of the importance of freedom of expression on the Internet. The Rapporteur emphasises the need for clear rules, in contrast with the arbitrariness he observes today, which allows for increasing surveillance and monitoring of communications.

Restrictions and regulations must be in accordance with Council of Europe standards, and in particular the ECHR and the case law of the Strasbourg Court concerning the narrow set of restrictions to freedom of expression necessary in a democratic society. Also, any interference with the rights to communicate, express views or assemble must be based on rules that are clear, specific and accessible. Given the crucial importance of these freedoms, such rules should to a large extent be written in statute law, which cannot be easily or quickly changed. To further prevent arbitrariness, any authority to which the power to apply the laws is delegated should be entirely independent, be required to give accessible, transparent and reasoned rulings, and be subject to judicial supervision.

Special attention should be paid to the concept of "incitement to violence", which should be interpreted in full and effective compliance with the standards in the ECHR and the case law of the Court. The report from the UN Special Rapporteur, for example, states that, on the important issue of the censorship of alleged support for terrorism, restrictions on the right to expression can only be justified if the government can demonstrate that the expression is intended to incite imminent violence, and that there is a direct and immediate connection between this expression and the likelihood or occurrence of such violence.

There is also a need to continue the discussion on how to ensure the protection of individual integrity (data protection) in social media without undermining the right to freedom of expression.

Conclusions

- Internet freedom is important. All restrictions must be based on clear, specific and accessible statute law;
- Those regulatory authorities applying the laws restricting freedom of expression must be entirely independent, accountable and with adequate safeguards in place to avoid arbitrariness;
- Greater transparency and proportionality of Internet blocking is required, including narrowing the grounds for restriction of prohibited content to those accepted by the case law of the Court, and publishing public lists of blocked sites;
- Blocking must be carried out with effective notice on the conclusion of due process, and interested parties should be given the opportunity to challenge the decision in public judicial proceedings.

Thomas Hammarberg
Council of Europe Commissioner for Human Rights
Strasbourg, 1 November 2011

Acknowledgement

Anki Wood played a key role in the production of this publication; advising and assisting the authors, organising the material, editing texts and overseeing the technical production.

Chapter 1:
Protection of journalists from violence

Dunja Mijatović, OSCE Representative on Freedom of the Media

> The right of journalists to carry out their work under safe conditions, without fear of being harassed, attacked, beaten or killed is of paramount importance for freedom of the press and freedom of expression.

Hrant Dink, a Turkish-Armenian journalist, was murdered in 2007. People began gathering where he was killed, in front of the Agos newspaper office, and did not leave the place for days. Flowers and candles covered the spot where he fell. The notes say: "Hrant Dink, we will never forget you. We strongly condemn this ugly attack." Photo © Hrant Dink Foundation.

Summary

Although the challenges and dangers that journalists face may differ from country to country, one sad fact holds true everywhere: their freedom to express themselves is questioned and challenged from many sides. Some of these challenges are blatant, others concealed; some of them use traditional methods to silence free speech and critical voices, some use new technologies to suppress and restrict the free flow of information and media pluralism; and far too many result in physical harassment and deadly violence against journalists.

The right of journalists to carry out their work under safe conditions, without fear of being harassed, attacked, beaten or killed is of paramount importance for freedom of the press and freedom of expression.

The aim of this chapter is to draw attention to the critical problems journalists face in their work – and to the responsibilities that we, as officials of international organisations, have to demand of the authorities, to ensure that journalists can work safely. Attempts to intimidate journalists are unfortunately very common. During the last five years close to 30 journalists were killed in the Organization for Security and Co-operation in Europe (OSCE) region[1] – and that number is far surpassed by those who were beaten up or whose lives were threatened.

The first section of this chapter describes the dangers of working as a journalist. The frequency with which journalists are harassed, attacked and murdered is a matter of grave concern. The threat of violence has become a form of censorship, which often goes unpunished. This section also discusses the danger of impunity: the blatant neglect of human rights when the authorities allow perpetrators to go unpunished. This sends a dangerous signal to society, and can lead to further violence.

---

1. The Organization for Security and Co-operation in Europe (OSCE) comprises 56 participating states over three continents – North America, Europe and Asia. See: www.osce.org.

The second section discusses the protection media professionals enjoy – or are meant to enjoy – under international humanitarian law. It also highlights the concern that, despite the several conventions that spell out everyone's right to freedom of expression, innumerable cases of violence with the aim of silencing journalists occur every year. Of the almost 30 murders of journalists in the OSCE region, successful prosecutions resulted in only about one tenth of cases. This casts serious doubts on the effectiveness of law enforcement bodies and the judiciary.

The third section focuses on what can be done to better protect journalists from violence. It requires strong commitment from governments, law enforcement agencies and legislators, as well as international organisations, civil society and journalists' organisations to secure progress in this area. The best results can be achieved if they work together.

Governments must understand why journalists need special attention. Violence against journalists is a crime against basic democratic values such as free expression and the right to information. Therefore governments need to commit themselves to treating such violence as crimes aimed at undermining public order and democratic governance. Appropriate amendments need to be introduced in criminal and civil laws. Governmental authorities, politicians and law enforcement agencies must treat these crimes with the full political, administrative and technical resources available to them so as to ensure the criminals involved, including those who ordered the crimes, do not escape justice.

There is no doubt that journalists ought to uphold the highest professional standards in order to defend the dignity of this noble profession. However, the level of professionalism employed must not be used as an argument by governments when discussing the safety of journalists or lack thereof. In too many regions, governments misconstrue the meaning of responsibility. It is often assumed that "responsible journalism" means "no criticism, no satire, no provocation, and no differing voices". This approach leads to self-censorship and presents a double-edged sword, suppressing and silencing voices. Governments should nurture an environment in which their citizens live in a society where free speech is protected by laws in order to foster, not suppress, pluralistic media. If these and other basic conditions for a free society are not provided for, journalists and the media will always look for alternative ways to loudly and clearly voice their opinions to shed light on issues of importance to society.

The overall conclusion is that safety of the media and media professionals is a precondition for free media. Without safe working conditions, journalists cannot write freely. To defend the very important human rights of free media and free expression, authorities and organisations at all levels need to combine their efforts.

Introduction

Journalism is an important profession. It can be seen as a skill, a talent, even a passion in a way: a passion to tell the truth, to inform, to reach others, to communicate news using any means necessary. So why is this passion, this profession, so fiercely attacked, challenged and perceived as controversial?

Many journalists have risked their futures, have been beaten, harassed, imprisoned and too many have even made the ultimate sacrifice – of their lives – in the pursuit of telling a story, exposing the truth and acknowledging the right to be heard. Along with threats directed to freedom of speech and freedom of the media in general, today the freedom to be a journalist is also threatened.

We do not always appreciate the importance of the universal right to free expression and free speech until they are tampered with by state interference and control. Without the expression of ideas and opinions and their publication and distribution in the media, no society can develop effectively. As citizens we should protect our freedom of speech and freedom of the media to ensure that all other human rights are protected.

Too many nations around the world know that, like democracy, freedom of the media and freedom of speech do not come naturally, and cannot be taken for granted. They must be constantly justified, reaffirmed and strengthened.

Governments can play a crucial role in creating a safe environment for journalists. Free and independent media are the cornerstone of a vibrant democratic society. Democracy flourishes when journalists are free to seek out and question all members of the public, particularly government officials, whose jobs rely on the public's trust.

Violence against journalists

At present safety may be the biggest issue for press freedom. The Committee to Protect Journalists reports that since 1992, more than 100 journalists in the Council of Europe region[2] have been killed because of their line of work, and many, many more have been physically attacked or have received threats.

The high number of violent attacks against journalists is cause for deep concern. Equally alarming is the authorities' willingness to classify many of the murders as unrelated to the journalist's professional activities. We also see that critical speech is being punished more frequently, with questionable charges being brought against journalists. The impunity of the perpetrators and the responsible authorities' passivity in investigating and failing to publicly condemn these murders breeds further violence.

There are many other forms of harassment or intimidation besides physical violence and imprisonment that also have a threatening effect on journalists. With the heightened security concerns of the last decade, police and prosecutors have increasingly raided editorial offices and journalists' homes or seized their equipment, while searching for leaks that were perceived to be national security threats.

---

2. The Council of Europe covers virtually the entire European continent, with its 47 member states. See: www.coe.int.

An extreme form of censorship

Hardly a year goes by without journalists in the OSCE region paying with their lives for writing about issues that they know will put them in danger. We are also very familiar with the numerous beatings that take place, often causing horrific injuries.

Today, in the 21st century, it is dangerous to be a journalist, a photographer or a member of the media. It is dangerous to be a journalist and to have lunch with a source in a restaurant. It is dangerous to be a friend or neighbour of a journalist. It is dangerous to write about corruption. It is dangerous to investigate stories. In many parts of the world it is dangerous to be a monitor of our times and it is dangerous to be a human being who speaks his or her mind freely.

If murder is the most extreme form of censorship, it is not the only form being practised. Throughout the region, journalists are beaten on a regular basis. Moreover, their attackers are often not caught or punished. Imprisonment also remains a very common way to quash free speech throughout the OSCE region; journalists are often put behind bars for practising their craft, which often involves reporting on corruption and corrupt public officials. In Turkey alone, more than 60 journalists are in prison; the authorities insist that most of them are convicted of crimes not related to their professional activities.

No one should fear being jailed for exposing the truth. As long as journalists are afraid for their lives and the lives of their families while doing their job, we do not live in a free society.

Journalists continue to die, not only when covering events on the battlefield, but also, and more often so, in the course of their work, trying to shine light on the darker sides of society: corruption, financial abuse, drug trafficking, terrorism and ethnic conflict, among others.[3] In 2009 in Vilnius, the OSCE Parliamentary Assembly also dealt with this problem, and passed a resolution on strengthening the

---

3. PACE Recommendation 1506 (2001). See: http://assembly.coe.int/Main.asp?link=/Documents/AdoptedText/ta01/EREC1506.htm.

OSCE's engagement on freedom of opinion and expression; it urged participating states to fully investigate criminal activities against journalists, particularly those aimed at intimidating journalists reporting independently, and to fully prosecute those responsible for these criminal activities.[4]

There are many journalists who stop writing critically on issues of importance. Often we do not know why. Apart from threats of physical harm, there are other, less visible forms of violence which can silence a journalist. There are countless situations where there are no bruises, no explosions and no lost lives; violence that creeps in more quietly, that is impossible to point out, is impossible to address directly. What can be done when a journalist stops writing because someone has asked if they knew where their son or daughter was at the time? Or if they want to see their family again?

This is psychological violence which results in trauma. Although less spoken about, it affects journalists every day. It can manifest itself in various ways, including intimidation, harassment or threats. You are intimidated for example if you are persistently followed by security agents, or if your home or editorial office is being watched, or if you are warned against doing something you have the right to do – such as writing an article that will expose wrongdoings in society. You can be harassed in person, over the phone, or in e-mails sent to you. All such cases have one thing in common – you do not know if, or when, these threats will become a reality. But they can make you fearful for your safety or for the safety of your loved ones.

Nations that do not allow independent media to examine the work, and wrongdoings, of officials who have a fiduciary duty to the public are harming their own development and prosperity. For this reason, in 1994 at the Budapest Summit of the Conference on Security and Co-operation in Europe, the participating states condemned "all attacks on and harassment of journalists", and committed themselves

---

4. Resolution on Strengthening OSCE Engagement on Freedom of Opinion and Expression, adopted by the OSCE Parliamentary Assembly in Vilnius in July 2009.

to "endeavour to hold those directly responsible for such attacks and harassment accountable."[5]

It is encouraging that as recently as December 2010, at the OSCE Summit in Astana, all 56 participating states confirmed that human rights and fundamental freedoms are inalienable, and underlined that their protection and promotion remain their primary responsibility. They reaffirmed categorically and irrevocably that the commitments undertaken in the field of the human dimension are matters of direct and legitimate concern to all participating states and do not belong exclusively to the internal affairs of the State concerned.[6]

Murders

While the commitment to protect freedom of the media is a noble goal, implementation has not been impressive so far. In the OSCE region, around 30 journalists are estimated to have been killed in the past five years alone – a number far surpassed by those who were beaten up or whose lives were threatened.

Of OSCE participating states, the Russian Federation is where most members of the media have been killed. The most publicised include Paul Klebnikov *(Forbes, Russia)*, Anna Politkovskaya *(Novaya Gazeta)*, Yury Shchekochikhin *(Novaya Gazeta)*, Vladislav Listyev *(ORT)* and Dmitry Kholodov *(Moskovsky Komsomolets)*. But let us also remember Ivan Safronov *(Kommersant)*, Vyacheslav Yaroshenko *(Korruptsiya i Prestupnost)*, Larisa Yudina *(Sovetskaya Kalmykiya Segodnya)*, Magomed Yevolyev *(Ingushetiya.ru)*, Nataya Skryl *(Nashe vremya)* and Valery Ivanov *(Tolyttinskoye obozrenoya)*, among many others.

In Ukraine, more than 10 years after Georgiy Gongadze's murder, the masterminds behind the crime are yet to be punished. However, it is commendable that there have been renewed efforts to investigate and punish all those involved. The authorities should consider all the evidence available to them and make sure they do their utmost to

---

5. See: www.osce.org/fom/31232, page 21.
6. See: www.osce.org/odihr/43677.

discover the truth about the circumstances of this murder and bring all those responsible for this horrible killing to justice. The Ukrainian Government is now faced with another test of its will: identifying and prosecuting those responsible for the August 2010 disappearance of Vasil Klymentyev, editor of *Novy Stil*.

We should also remember the murders (some of which remain unsolved) of Elmar Huseynov *(Monitor)* who was killed in Azerbaijan in 2005; Slavko Ćuruvija *(Dnevni Telegraf)* and Milan Pantić *(Vecernje Novosti)* who were murdered in Serbia in 1999 and 2001 respectively; and Ivo Pukanić *(Nacional)* and his marketing director, Niko Franjić, who were killed by a car bomb in Croatia in 2008.

In Turkey, too, there have been cases that must not be forgotten. The murder of Hrant Dink, a Turkish-Armenian journalist who was shot in 2007, has raised many questions. Shortly after the murder a 17-year-old was arrested and later convicted of the crime. While he confessed to pulling the trigger, it is suspected that the real instigators behind Dink's death are yet to be brought to justice.

These incidents represent just a small proportion of the most serious crimes committed against journalists, and shed light on the disturbing state of media freedom in many countries within the OSCE region.

Physical attacks

In the last year alone, there have been innumerable attempts to intimidate journalists in the OSCE region. In Belarus for instance, the post-election violence in December 2010 against members of the foreign and Belarusian press corps shocked the world. In November 2010 in the Russian Federation, Oleg Kashin of the daily *Kommersant* was brutally attacked in Moscow by unidentified individuals. In Bulgaria in February 2011 there was an explosion just outside the Sofia office of the *Galeria* weekly. During the same month poster-sized death notices were pasted around the town of Lazarevac, Serbia, listing the names of prominent B92 journalists. In July 2010, Teofil Pančić, a political columnist for the Serbian weekly *Vreme* known for his critical coverage of Serbian nationalists and sports hooligans, was physically attacked in public. During July and August 2011, four delivery vehicles were set on fire in front of the office of the newspaper *Vijesti* in Podgorica, Montenegro. A total of three attacks against the *Vijesti* newspaper had occurred within two months, exerting a "chilling effect" on all journalists in Montenegro.

Two of the most prominent Turkish journalists to be harassed in this manner are Nedim Şener and Ahmet Şık. Both are facing criminal charges in a number of trials, and have been in pre-trial detention since March of this year in the well-known *Ergenekon* case.

In France, in January 2011, Michaël Szames (*France 24*) was allegedly the victim of a violent attack. The reporter filed a complaint with the police accusing eight security staff of the National Front Party of having beaten and insulted him as he was covering a party congress.

In the same month, there was a case in Spain where Fernando Santiago, President of the Press Association of Cadiz, was brutally attacked in response to a newspaper article about the use of public funds to rescue Delphi, a struggling automobile parts company.

Earlier in the year, Fabio Cosmo Colombo, a journalist for the Italian newspaper *Metropolis*, was attacked and left unconscious, while police allegedly looked on but did not intervene. Colombo was reporting on the death of a young man – later declared a suicide – when the attack took place.

Still, journalists across the OSCE region continue to carry out their jobs and to provide the public with the news necessary in a democratic society.

Impunity

Soon after the murder of Anna Politkovskaya, the suspected killer was identified. He fled the country and was only recently arrested in Chechnya. However, several others accused of involvement in the murder had been apprehended earlier. Two brothers and a former officer from the organised crime squad went on trial accused of having helped to organise the killing. The prosecution also alleged that a serving officer from the FSB, the Russian intelligence service, had played a major part in planning Politkovskaya's assassination.

Three years after the murder, in February 2009, all four were acquitted and immediately released. The prosecution objected to the acquittals. Later the same year, the Russian Supreme Court upheld the prosecution's complaint and ordered a new trial, which is still pending. The suspected mastermind of Politkovskaya's murder, a former Interior Ministry official, was arrested in August this year. However, to date no one has been sentenced by a court for the murder.

Impunity has become a key word in understanding the state of the press in Europe. Impunity is the blatant neglect of human rights by the authorities, which allows the perpetrators to remain unpunished. Over the years we have witnessed the unwillingness of authorities to confirm that murders are related to journalistic activities. As a result, investigations are not swift, thorough or successful in many OSCE countries.

This sends a depressing message, not only to all those concerned with protecting free expression and media freedom. In aiming to intimidate investigative and political journalists, it sends a dangerous signal to society that it cannot rely on the courage of the press to report on the wrongdoings of the powers that be, to expose corruption and to change life for the better. This develops into a "vicious circle" when passive acceptance by the public authorities only leads to more bloodshed and less journalism. Such trends undermine security and co-operation in a nation; in the end they undermine security and co-operation in Europe.

Miklós Haraszti, my distinguished predecessor, recently said: "Impunity breeds further violence, and practically blesses the most brutal type of censorship without saying so."

Unfortunately, today's media in much of the OSCE area do not have much hope that the murders of their colleagues will result in swift and successful prosecutions. Most perpetrators of such crimes have not been brought to justice, which casts serious doubts on the effectiveness of law enforcement bodies and of the judiciary. Very often this is not an issue relating to their competence and training, but rather of the willingness of the authorities to disclose the truth.

Of the almost 30 murders of journalists in the OSCE region since 2007, only one tenth were followed by the arrest of suspects and their successful prosecutions. No doubt there are many reasons for these failures, but whether it is prosecutorial passivity or lack of resources, this sends the wrong message to society and, equally important, to those who committed the crimes. This of course can lead to further violence and breeds an atmosphere of passive acceptance of these attacks.

Legal standards relating to the protection of journalism

Freedom of opinion and expression are acknowledged as human rights in international human rights law and in other international standards. These rights are enshrined in the Universal Declaration of Human Rights,[7] the European Convention on Human Rights (ECHR),[8] the Charter of Fundamental Rights of the European Union[9] and in the International Covenant on Civil and Political Rights.[10]

---

7. Universal Declaration of Human Rights, Article 19:
Everyone has the right to freedom of opinion and expression; this right includes freedom to hold opinions without interference and to seek, receive and impart information and ideas through any media and regardless of frontiers.
8. European Convention on Human Rights, Article 10: Freedom of expression, 1. Everyone has the right to freedom of expression. This right shall include freedom to hold opinions and to receive and impart information and ideas without interference by public authority and regardless of frontiers.
9. Charter of Fundamental Rights of the European Union, Article 11: Freedom of expression and information, 1. Everyone has the right to freedom of expression. This right shall include freedom to hold opinions and to receive and impart information and ideas without interference by public authority and regardless of frontiers.
10. International Covenant on Civil and Political Rights, Article 19: 1. Everyone shall have the right to hold opinions without interference. 2. Everyone shall have the right to freedom of expression; this right shall include freedom to seek, receive and impart information and ideas of all kinds, regardless of frontiers, either orally, in writing or in print, in the form of art, or through any other media of his choice.

In addition, the ECHR, in Article 2, protects the right to life. The European Court of Human Rights has repeatedly stated that the first sentence of Article 2, paragraph 1, "enjoins the State not only to refrain from the intentional and unlawful taking of life, but also to take appropriate steps to safeguard the lives of those within its jurisdiction".[11] According to the Court, Article 2 also requires that there be some form of effective official investigation when individuals have been killed by the use of force.

The Court found for instance that there had been a violation of Article 2 following the authorities' failure to protect the life of Georgiy Gongadze. Moreover, the Court considered that, during the investigation, the authorities were more preoccupied with proving the lack of involvement of high-level state officials in the case than discovering the truth about the circumstances of Gongadze's disappearance and death. The Court therefore concluded that there had been a violation of Article 2 concerning the failure to conduct an effective investigation into the case.

In 2010, the Court issued a judgment in the case of *Dink v. Turkey*.[12] The Court concluded that by abandoning the criminal proceedings against the responsible policemen (for negligence in the protection of Hrant Dink's life), the government had been in breach of its obligation to protect Dink's right to life. More recently, two officers and four non-commissioned officers of the Turkish Gendarmerie were sentenced for negligence and failure to act on intelligence on Dink's potential assassination.

---

11. See for instance the case of *Gongadze v. Ukraine*, Appl. No. 34056/02, judgment of 8 November 2005, paragraph 164. The Court added: "This involves a primary duty on the State to secure the right to life by putting in place effective criminal-law provisions to deter the commission of offences against the person, backed up by law enforcement machinery for the prevention, suppression and punishment of breaches of such provisions. It also extends, in appropriate circumstances, to a positive obligation on the authorities to take preventive operational measures to protect an individual or individuals whose lives are at risk from the criminal acts of another individual."
12. *Dink v. Turkey*, Appl. Nos. 2668/07, 6102/08, 30079/08, 7072/09 and 7124/09, judgment of 14 September 2010.

Practical guarantees of non-disclosure of the confidential sources of journalists are also a tool to minimise the risks associated with the profession. In 1996, the Court stated that:

> *Protection of journalistic sources is one of the basic conditions for press freedom ... Without such protection, sources may be deterred from assisting the press in informing the public on matters of public interest. As a result the vital public-watchdog role of the press may be undermined and the ability of the press to provide accurate and reliable information may be adversely affected.*[13]

The Court concluded that in the absence of "an overriding requirement in the public interest", an order to disclose sources would violate the guarantee of free expression enshrined in Article 10 of the ECHR.

This case led the Council of Europe's Committee of Ministers to adopt Recommendation No. R (2000) 7 on the right of journalists not to disclose their sources of information. This recommendation gives guidance as to how member states should implement the protection of sources in their domestic legislation. More recently the Parliamentary Assembly of the Council of Europe adopted Recommendation 1950 (2011) on the protection of journalists' sources. In my capacity as the OSCE Representative on Freedom of the Media, I have also called on several participating states to respect this right.

Defamation to silence the media

Charges of defamation continue to put journalists in many participating states behind bars. The fact that these offences are still part of criminal law in many western European countries (even if they have not been applied for decades) means that the chilling effect of the possibility of imprisonment for published or broadcast words continues to curb free expression. Here "old democracies" provide a bad example to countries in transition. We all must realise that when we speak of the sanctions for defamatory and other potentially harmful

---

13. *Goodwin v. the United Kingdom*, Appl. No. 17488/90, judgment of 27 March 1996, para. 39. See also *Sanoma Uitgevers B.V. v. the Netherlands*, Appl. No. 38224/03, judgment of 14 September 2010.

materials and publications that journalists are not equal to everyone else in this regard: like public servants, policemen and diplomats, they serve society at large, they protect democracy, and in the line of duty they should enjoy special protection and privileges themselves.

The decriminalisation of defamation is an essential step for the protection of freedom of expression, and any reform should follow the standards established by the Court.

The Court has underlined in several cases that "the imposition of a prison sentence for a press offence will be compatible with journalists' freedom of expression as guaranteed by Article 10 of the ECHR only in exceptional circumstances, notably where other fundamental rights have been seriously impaired, as, for example, in cases of hate speech or incitement to violence".[14]

So far 13 OSCE participating states have decriminalised libel and defamation; most of them carried out this very important reform quite recently.[15]

It is of paramount importance that journalists not be imprisoned for their words, for their professional activities, for insults or for slander. There are sufficient sanctions in administrative and civil law for justice to prevail in defamation conflicts – although sanctions must be appropriate and proportionate.

Protection of journalists from violence

Violence with the aim to silence journalists can take many forms, from physical attacks to verbal threats. Public authorities, civil society and the international community, as well as media owners and journalists' organisations, all have important roles to play in ensuring the

---

14. *Mahmudov and Agazade v. Azerbaijan*, Appl. No. 35877/04, judgment of 18 December 2008, paragraph 50.
15. The 13 participating states in the OSCE region who, as per 11 July 2011, had fully decriminalised defamation are Armenia, Bosnia and Herzegovina, Cyprus, Estonia, Georgia, Kyrgyzstan, Moldova, Romania, Ireland, United Kingdom, Ukraine, Montenegro and the USA.

safety of journalists. There are some encouraging examples of how different actors have worked together in order to protect journalists under threat.

In 2007 Eynulla Fatullayev, an Azerbaijani journalist and editor of independent newspapers in Baku, was sentenced to prison on defamation charges in relation to an Internet posting on a 1992 massacre during the Nagorno-Karabakh conflict. His release in May 2011 was preceded by a number of international activities.

In 2009 the Committee to Protect Journalists honoured Fatullayev with its annual International Press Freedom Award for "defending press freedom in the face of attacks, threats or imprisonment".

In the course of a visit to Azerbaijan in March 2010 the Council of Europe Commissioner for Human Rights visited Fatullayev in the detention centre where he was held. The Commissioner urged the authorities to release him without delay and stressed that all journalists and any other persons imprisoned because of views or opinions expressed should be released immediately.[16] I also visited him in my capacity as the OSCE Representative on Freedom of the Media, and so did my predecessor, Miklós Haraszti. My office, as well as many non-governmental organisations (NGOs), had been putting considerable efforts into his release from prison over the years.

In a judgment of 22 April 2010,[17] the Court concluded that there had been two violations of Article 10 of the ECHR, as well as a violation of Article 6, paragraph 1 (his case was not heard by an independent tribunal) and paragraph 2 (violation of the presumption of innocence). Moreover, the Court found it unacceptable that Fatullayev still remained imprisoned and called upon the Azerbaijani authorities to secure his immediate release, in order to put an end to the violations of Article 10 of the ECHR.

---

16. See: Report by Thomas Hammarberg, Commissioner for Human Rights of the Council of Europe, following his visit to Azerbaijan from 1 to 5 March 2010: https://wcd.coe.int/wcd/ViewDoc.jsp?id=1642017&Site=CommDH&BackColorInternet=FEC65B&BackColorIntranet=FEC65B&BackColorLogged=FFC679.

17. *Fatullayev v. Azerbaijan*, Appl. No. 40984/07, judgment of 22 April 2010.

In May 2011 I visited Azerbaijan in my role as OSCE Representative on Freedom of the Media. I met with President Ilham Aliyev and top officials in Baku, in order to voice concerns regarding media freedom in the country and to call again on the authorities to free Fatullayev.

On 24 May 2011, UK journalists including Jon Snow of Channel 4 News and John Mulholland, editor of *The Observer*, joined Amnesty International in issuing a "mass tweet" on Fatullayev's behalf: the journalists photographed themselves with placards reading "Free Eynulla Fatullayev!" and tweeted the photos to President Aliyev.

Fatullayev received a full pardon two days later, and was released after serving four years of his eight-year sentence. He attributed his release to the work of the activists, saying, "In my opinion, you saved me. Thank you to all those who tweeted." This is a vivid example of what Commissioner Hammarberg calls mobilisation of "effective pressure".

Another example of a joint effort is the release from detention of the Tajik journalist Urunbek Usmonov in July 2011, which was a result of an outcry by international organisations, but also of protests by numerous citizen groups and media outlets – including his employer, the British Broadcasting Corporation.

In order to make progress in better protecting journalists, we need to be realistic and open about the problems we currently face in many countries, and aware of what kind of protection journalists need. Professor Mikhail Fedotov, Chairman of the Council of the President of the Russian Federation on Development of Civil Society and Human Rights, has described the main components of journalists' safety to be the following: physical safety, legal safety, information safety, economic safety and psychological safety.[18]

---

18. See: www.osce.org/fom/78737. Journalism Between Safety and Impunity. Presentation by Prof. Mikhail Fedotov, Chairman, Council of the President of the Russian Federation on Development of Civil Society and Human Rights at the Conference on Safety of Journalists in the OSCE Region, Vilnius, 7 June 2011.

It takes strong commitment and co-operation from governments, international organisations, civil society, the media industry and journalists' own organisations to cover all these areas.

Responses from journalists' organisations, the media industry and NGOs

The phenomenon of attacks on journalists is nothing new. However, what we do not usually hear is that, in some instances, attacks against journalists actually make the media community stronger, not weaker; it makes them braver, not more passive. There are a number of methods that have been used to strengthen the right of journalists to carry out their work under safe conditions.

Journalists' organisations can work proactively by:
- monitoring employers' actions regarding protection;
- training journalists concerning their rights and security measures;
- showing solidarity and exchanging experiences;
- giving input to the drafting of media legislation;
- providing legal support for journalists in conflict with their employers.

The owners – the media industry – obviously have a special obligation to support and protect their employees. Their safety precautions should include:
- assessing the level of danger together with the journalist in question;
- providing security arrangements for journalists working on sensitive cases or who are on dangerous missions, such as individual protection equipment and emergency communication means;
- special training;
- additional insurance for journalists in conflict zones or in danger;
- observing the social and labour rights of journalists;
- debriefing and support, both before and after an assignment;
- not assigning journalists to illegal editorial missions, as these not only put reporters in danger, but also tarnish the profession.

There are several NGOs that play a vital role in the protection of journalists against violence by:

- monitoring cases of violence and threats;
- collecting and disseminating information in reports and press releases;
- engaging the public;
- demanding answers and results from the authorities and others concerned;
- providing an impact on the legislative process;
- creating a public consensus and understanding for the role of journalism and media in modern society.

Some examples of prominent organisations working with issues of media freedom are:

- Amnesty International
- ARTICLE 19
- Reporters without Borders
- Association of European Journalists
- Center for Journalism in Extreme Situations
- Committee to Protect Journalists
- European Newspaper Publishers' Association
- Freedom House
- The International Federation of Journalists
- International Press Institute
- South East Europe Media Organisation.

In parallel with their own proactive work, international and national human rights and media organisations – media business organisations as well as unions – can forge alliances that actively and in different ways identify and prevent violations of media freedom.

Regarding new media and citizen journalism, the strategies to increase safety are the same. When monitoring media freedom problems, we do not determine who is a journalist; we simply look at the human right to free expression. Citizen journalists are more numerous than professionals and sometimes more united – here lies their strength vis-à-vis threats and intimidation.

In a way, guarantees of the freedom and safety of journalists lie not only in politics and law but also in technology. The very existence of open telecommunications networks, of Twitter and other social networks on the Internet, is creating a new environment for traditional media as some of the restrictions on them are rendered pointless by the spread of new technologies.

Counterbalancing state interference

Self-regulation, good ethics and an exchange of best practices are good methods to protect the media from government "lessons" and to counterbalance state interference. They are usually effective, and also have positive effects on journalism itself.

Strong self-regulation mechanisms, such as press councils, build public trust for the media and strengthen solidarity among journalists, at least among responsible journalists. At the same time self-regulation is a double-edged sword: to be effective the process has to be owned by the journalists – or, at least, journalists must be loyal to the idea. Alas, this has not worked in many countries, no matter what part of Europe we look at.

Education and training, including a legal component, is another strong instrument to protect journalists. Joint training of journalists and judges to counter mutual mistrust is welcome. Best practices in one participating state should be shared among professionals. Here we rely on the support of the media business.

Responses from international organisations

Through monitoring, setting universal standards and giving assistance, international organisations can enhance the general conditions for the safety of journalists – especially when they all work towards a common goal. Two international organisations in Europe devoted to this are the OSCE and the Council of Europe.

The Office of the OSCE Representative on Freedom of the Media

The safety of journalists is the main focus of the Office of the OSCE Representative on Freedom of the Media. Ever since it was created in 1997, this institution has been drawing attention to the alarming increase in violent attacks against journalists. Its mandate is to remind the 56 participating states to live up to the set of commitments to uphold and foster media freedom that they agreed to as members of the OSCE. In declaration after declaration, dating back to the Helsinki Accords of 1975, the nations that make up the OSCE have agreed to create societies that respect the universal right to free expression and free speech.

The OSCE commitments oblige all participating states to provide safety to journalists, not just for the sake of justice but also for the sake of democracy, which is just a meaningless word without fearless fact-finding and discussion by and within the media. Unfortunately, the practice in many countries falls far short of the ideal.

Council of Europe institutions

Various Council of Europe bodies are contributing to ensuring free and independent media, as enshrined in the ECHR of 1950.[19]

The issue is a priority theme for the Office of the Commissioner for Human Rights. The Commissioner gathers information, identifies shortcomings and provides advice on ways to improve media freedom and the protection of journalists. He also supports initiatives aimed at strengthening media professionalism and ethical journalism and the establishment of self-regulatory mechanisms.[20]

In its Recommendation 1897 (2010) on respect for media freedom the Parliamentary Assembly of the Council of Europe noted "with great concern" that the number of attacks on the media and journalists and other serious violations of media freedom have increased.

---

19. See: www.coe.int/lportal/web/coe-portal/what-we-do/media-and-communication/media-freedom?dynLink=true&layoutId=42&dlgroupId=10226&fromArticleId.
20. See: www.coe.int/t/commissioner/activities/themes/MediaFreedom/Default_en.asp.

The Assembly recommended that the Committee of Ministers assist member states in training their judges, law enforcement authorities and police in respecting media freedom, in particular as regards the protection of journalists and media against violent threats. The Assembly also encouraged the Secretary General of the Council of Europe to set up continuous monitoring on media freedom violations in member states, using information from journalists and human rights groups.[21]

Responses from governments

I am pleased to state that there is also good news to report when looking at governmental reactions to violence against journalists. We saw the swift condemnation in the summer of 2010 by the Greek authorities of the killing of Sokratis Giokias as well as the instigation of an investigation into the case.

In Serbia Veran Matić, journalist and editor-in-chief of the Belgrade-based television station *B92*, is under 24-hour police protection. The same kind of police protection is being provided to Brankica Stanković, another *B92* journalist, due to ongoing concerns for her security.

The Criminal Code of Serbia was amended in 2009 to introduce "endangering of the safety of a journalist" as a crime punishable by imprisonment ranging from one to eight years. This provision was applied for the first time in 2010 when three persons were convicted for threatening Brankica Stanković. In August 2010, I welcomed the Serbian Government's swift investigation into the attacks against her and Teofil Pančić, political columnist for the weekly *Vreme*.

In Russia, where many problems have festered over the past 20 years, it is especially heartening to learn that top government authorities are taking a proactive role in solving murder cases against journalists. Another encouraging example is that of Aleksandr Bastrykin, the head of the Investigative Committee, who has ordered a review of all criminal cases opened in relation to attacks against the media,

---

21. See: http://assembly.coe.int/Mainf.asp?link=/Documents/AdoptedText/ta10/EREC1897.htm.

with special attention to cases that were closed or suspended before the creation of the committee he heads.

The successful prosecutions of those who killed journalist Igor Domnikov (*Novaya Gazeta*), journalist Anastasia Baburova (*Novaya Gazeta*) and human rights lawyer Stanislav Markelov are welcome. While the latter case is now on appeal, the verdicts give hope to society as a whole and prove that crime will not go unpunished. This is the right way forward.

Governments must understand why violence against journalists is not an ordinary crime. It is a crime against democratic values. All states need to commit themselves to treating violence against journalists as a crime aimed at undermining public order and democratic governance. However, rhetoric is not enough. Dynamic words do not always translate into dynamic action. What we need to achieve is the transformation of these dignified goals into concrete and effective action.

Appropriate amendments need to be made to criminal law. Governmental authorities, politicians and law enforcement agencies must treat these crimes with the full political, administrative and technical resources available to them to make sure the criminals who have planned and carried out attacks on journalists do not escape justice.

Conclusions

Violence against journalists – whether murder, physical harm or psychological violence – remains a special category of crime, as it is a direct attack on society and democracy itself. As such, it must be met with harsh condemnation and prosecution. The professional activity of a journalist who has been the victim of a violent crime must be taken into consideration and cases must be investigated as a priority.

However, most perpetrators of such crimes have not been brought to justice, which casts serious doubts on the effectiveness of the law enforcement bodies and judiciary. Very often this is not an issue related to their competence and training, but rather of the willingness of the authorities to uncover the truth.

Of the almost 30 murders that have taken place in the OSCE region in the last five years, only one tenth were followed by the arrest of suspects and their successful prosecutions. This is not acceptable. The reasons for this failure could be numerous, including prosecutorial passivity or lack of resources, but what it amounts to is a very unfortunate message to society and, equally important, to those who committed the crimes.

It is also of paramount importance that journalists not be imprisoned for their words, for their professional activities, for insults or for slander. There are sufficient sanctions in administrative and civil law for justice to prevail in defamation conflicts.

While the 56 participating states of the OSCE have long ago recognised the necessity of free media in a democracy, a positive climate only appears when governments themselves show more openness and more tolerance towards critical or dissenting views. Public officials must be able to accept a higher level of criticism, without considering it a threat to national security or a form of extremist activity. It is also important for them to acknowledge the work of journalists, to pay more respect and thus grant more dignity to the profession.

Guarantees of the freedom of the media involve three sets of commitments which governments have to make. The authorities should:

–   not interfere with freedom of the media in contradiction with agreed international human rights standards;

–   protect people pursuing this profession from being harassed and exposed to violence;

–   develop the conditions in which free media and freedom of expression can flourish. This is perhaps the hardest and most complex commitment. A basic foundation for this is a full recognition that the safety of journalists and journalism is an absolute prerequisite for democracy.

The Strasbourg Court has made it clear that governments have an obligation (under the ECHR) to protect the lives of threatened journalists and that murders of media professionals need to be investigated, prosecuted, tried and punished. No effort must be spared in apprehending and bringing to justice not only the actual killers, but also those who order these murders. Only if all this is taken seriously is it possible to break the vicious cycle of impunity.

Many NGOs, international organisations and media organisations are committed to – and work together – ensuring better implementation of these commitments. But it is only with the support and commitment of governments and the authorities that we will see less intimidation and more freedom in this very noble profession.

Chapter 2:
Ethical journalism and human rights

**Aidan White, international media specialist and former General
Secretary of the International Federation of Journalists**

> The aim is to create a modern vision of journalism,
> one that suits the age. Such a vision would revive
> the notion of mission in journalism, and appeal to
> idealism and dedication to principles that nourish
> democracy and respect for human rights, not just in
> the media but across the whole of society.

Photo © Shutterstock.

Summary

Ethical journalism concerns the way in which reporters, editors and others provide commentary on the events that shape people's lives. It is rooted in moral values and has evolved hand in hand with human rights protection in Europe over 150 years. Today journalism and human rights intersect at a moment of remarkable and historical change as a result of globalisation and the explosion of digital media.

The aim of this chapter is to set out a framework for fresh discussion of the ethical challenges that create tension between human rights and journalism.

The first section highlights the close relationship between the ethics of journalism and human rights standards. It points out that journalists, at least as much as governments, have a vested interest in the defence and promotion of high standards of human rights.

Section two examines the spectacular advances made in digital media and new forms of communication, such as "networked journalism". At the same time the notion of journalism as a public good is under pressure and in many European countries the independence of existing public media is not secure. This is a challenging context which requires reflection and action from journalists and states, guided by human rights principles.

Section three focuses on a number of major legal restraints on journalism, and examines current state practice and the development of relevant human rights law, notably through the European Convention on Human Rights (ECHR) and the European Court of Human Rights' case law.

The fourth section deals with the practical means through which ethical journalism may materialise: codes of conduct for journalists and self-regulation. Codes reflect the aspirations of journalists to be responsible and accountable. However, they need to be complemented by detailed guidelines and training that should be developed by media professionals with the support of states. Also, self-regulation of the media is presented as a valuable means of resolving conflicts, protecting the independence of journalism, promoting ethical standards and reducing the risk of legal sanctions against journalists.

The final substantive section refers to a number of important initiatives that aim to promote actively ethical standards of journalism and the protection of human rights on international, European or national levels, and may serve as examples for further good practice.

Introduction

In the mid-19th century, when Jean-Henri Dunant was crystallising his vision of humanity in times of war (embodied in the Red Cross and the Geneva Conventions), leading European editors were articulating ethical principles for their newspapers. A hundred years later, in the same year that the ECHR was adopted, the International Federation of Journalists agreed on the first international code of principles for the conduct of ethical journalism.

Today journalism and human rights once again intersect at a moment of remarkable and historical change as a result of globalisation and the explosion of digital media. It is, therefore, a good moment to develop a new narrative about the importance of ethical information and how European society is informed. In doing so we may also open the door to wider analysis of the ethical environment in which we live both as public and private citizens.

This chapter examines the tensions between the competing visions of human rights and ethical journalism. It does so through a critical prism, but it is not the intention to focus on differences between how rights are balanced, either in the newsroom or in the courtroom. Instead the aim is to embrace the positive relationship between these rights.

The objectives are two-fold, to:
- identify the practical steps needed to strengthen the conditions for the exercise of ethical journalism;
- raise awareness of the importance of ethical journalism and human rights protection and how, together, they can contribute to a better society.

Reporters and editors are not the mouthpiece of government, corporate power or even human rights defenders. At their best, journalists who aspire to tell stories based upon truth-telling, accuracy and fairness; who seek to minimise harm; and who make themselves accountable, define the essential elements of what we might call journalism as a public good.

Good journalism raises awareness of what is acceptable and unacceptable, and can remind us of moral responsibilities. It can reinforce our attachment to acceptable standards of behaviour and, in this sense, it is an ally of everyone striving for democracy and human rights protection.

Human rights standards relevant for journalism

Human rights are enshrined in the treaties between states, particularly the Universal Declaration of Human Rights (UDHR, 1948), the International Covenant on Civil and Political Rights (ICCPR, 1966) and the ECHR (1950), which guarantee the rights of all persons within the jurisdiction of the contracting parties. These rights are enshrined in law and in practice, as with the exercise of journalism, they are closely linked to the moral climate in which we live.

Journalists themselves have a vested interest in the defence and promotion of high standards of human rights, particularly the right to free expression under Article 19 of the UDHR and the ICCPR and Article 10 of the ECHR. The right to free expression also forms part of the Charter of Fundamental Rights of the European Union, in Article 11.

The case law related to free expression has been developed by the Strasbourg Court which has, over the years, provided important support in the fight for press freedom, particularly in relation to violations of Article 10 of the ECHR which provides the right to freedom of expression subject to certain restrictions that are "in accordance with law" and "necessary in a democratic society". This right includes the freedom to hold opinions, and to receive and impart information and ideas.

But this is a qualified right and may be overridden by decisions taken in the interest of national security, prevention of disorder or crime, or protection of an individual's reputation.

It is these potential limitations that worry journalists, who object to laws that provide unacceptably broad definitions of what constitutes "security" or "disorder" or "reputation", which can limit free speech, increase self-censorship and reduce legitimate scrutiny of public affairs.

Of course, human rights are sometimes conflicting. The need to balance competing rights provides potential traps for lawmakers and journalists alike. Article 10 of the ECHR, for instance, has to be balanced with Article 8, which sets out what has become the definition of the right to privacy in stating that "Everyone has the right to respect for his private and family life, his home and his correspondence."

When freedom of speech comes into conflict with other rights, such as the individual right to privacy, there is no easy way to make judgments, either in the courtroom or the newsroom, without giving one priority over the other.

In order to be able to make judgments that are morally and legally defensible, journalists must be competent, well trained, informed and, above all, able to operate freely in conditions which encourage them to act ethically. However, none of this is easily achieved in the pressurised and turbulent world in which the media work.

The new media landscape and the changes for journalism

Today journalism is in the midst of crisis. The traditional media, particularly newspapers, suffer not just from the effects of the global economic crisis but also the impact of structural and market changes which have reduced the profitability of media enterprises. In response to these changing fortunes, severe cuts have been imposed in editorial departments that have weakened the quality of journalism. Indeed, many media employers have sacrificed reporting standards in pursuit of commercial objectives, overriding ethical values with journalism that is populist, sensational and biased.[22]

In journalism the pain of this change is palpable. Many thousands of jobs have been eliminated, investment in training and investigative journalism has been cut, and there is precious little time, if any, for research, checking and original investigation.

In these conditions minorities are rendered invisible, their voices unheard; racist and xenophobic messages of unscrupulous politicians are increasingly in play; privacy is breached; there is scant analysis of issues like migration, religious and cultural differences; and little attempt to relieve the anxieties of societies troubled by economic and social dislocation.

The democratic consequences of this are clear: scrutiny of power, particularly at local and regional level, is much reduced and human rights protection is weakened.

In the midst of an information revolution we enjoy far greater opportunities for free expression and knowledge sharing; however, there are still concerns about the use and abuse of information.

New forms of communication and online services provide fresh challenges. So-called "citizen journalism" and the growth of "networked journalism" legitimise the use of amateurs in a weakened media industry and also pose new questions about the reliability and integrity of the information they provide.

Increasingly, there is pressure on states to intervene to support the media and responsible journalism, either by providing public money and subsidies to support failing independent media and the continuation of public interest journalism or to reinforce rules about media ownership in favour of transparency and pluralism.

Within journalism there are also new debates about reinforcing quality and objectivity within public service media and not least about

---

22. See: OECD (2010), *News in the Internet age: New trends in news publishing*, OECD Publishing, Paris and IFJ (2010), "Journalism: In touch with the future", Brussels.

guaranteeing editorial independence. In some countries such media, particularly broadcasting, are seen as instruments of propaganda. Confidence in public media is very low. This was acknowledged at the ministerial meeting of the Council of Europe on media held in Iceland in May 2009 which called for more editorial freedom and increased investment in new technologies.[23]

While journalists worry about their future and policymakers wrestle with questions of policy, the febrile atmosphere in which the media now work, defined by a 24-hour multi-platform news market, reinforces uncertainty about its role in supplying information.

But even though the Internet has opened up access to a superabundance of information, people still turn to trusted media brands and serious journalism for what they need most – fact-based information, analysis and context presented in digestible and bite-sized chunks. The WikiLeaks disclosures at the end of 2010, when distinguished journalists with five of the world's leading newspapers[24] were asked to filter thousands of detailed documents leaked from diplomatic sources in the United States of America, proved beyond doubt the continuing and vital role of editorial professionals in an open information environment.

Ethical journalism is needed even more at a time when people are increasingly overwhelmed by a glut of information, much of it impenetrable and most of which they cannot trust. People struggle to identify what is truthful and trustworthy. They are exposed to torrents of information that can be trivial, unreliable and irresponsible. There are fears over privacy and the loss of anonymity. Many fear the consequences for democracy of intrusive technologies in the hands of powerful political and corporate forces whose interests are not to embrace the positive potential of free expression, but to restrict dissent.

For journalists, governments and the public at large the task is to balance and protect rights while embracing the positive values of change,

---

23. 1st Council of Europe Conference of Ministers Responsible for Media and New Communications Services. "A new notion of media?" (28 to 29 May 2009, Reykjavik, Iceland). See: www.coe.int/t/dghl/standardsetting/media/doc/ConfMin_Address_Estonia_en.pdf.
24. *The New York Times, The Guardian, El País, Le Monde* and *Der Spiegel.*

but how is that to be done when the tendency is towards fractured, anonymous communications?

In the search for an answer it is useful to recall that the right to freedom of expression, as set out in Article 10 of the ECHR, covers a multitude of forms of expression. Journalists see their role in the context of press freedom, a form of expression that supports the discovery of truth. It is embedded in discussion in which different opinions are not only expressed, but are tested in open debate.

Freedom of expression in the widest sense does not support the discovery of truth. It gives everyone a right, within narrowly defined legal limits, to say what they want, how they want and when they want. They have the right to be decent or indecent, honest or dishonest, fair or biased. It is the right to be, in the words of philosopher Onora O'Neill, "self-regarding".[25]

Professionalism in journalism is conversely "other regarding". It is framed by the ethics of journalistic mission – truth-telling, independence and responsibility to others. Ethical journalism is about constrained expression, not free expression. It is about professionals who impose self-restraint based upon respect for others and attachment to ethical principles.

But to do this with any conviction journalists must be able to work free from pressure and intimidation. For this reason journalists, as much as governments, have a vested interest in the defence and promotion of high standards of human rights.

In many European countries the independence of media is not secure and journalists are routinely put under pressure. In some, journalists are victims of violence and impunity; in others they suffer forms of judicial intimidation.

Over the past 20 years, for instance, more than 2 000 journalists have been targeted and murdered worldwide. Some of Europe's most distinguished writers and journalists have been killed, many of them

---

25. See: O'Neill O. "A right to offend?", *The Guardian*, 13 February 2006, www.guardian.co.uk/media/2006/feb/13/mondaymediasection7.

victims of political enemies when alive and victims of governmental indifference in death, with evidence of widespread impunity.[26]

Journalists are also hampered by limits on their freedom imposed by undue political or corporate influence or by the application of law. This stifling atmosphere not only leads to self-censorship, it can intimidate and silence the sources upon which journalism depends.

This worrying climate has been reflected in recent discussions over media regulation, notably in the controversy over changes to media law in Hungary during 2010 when the government established a politically driven national media council to monitor and regulate journalism. This prompted an unprecedented intervention by the European Commission and led to calls from the European Parliament for media policies to be linked to enhanced co-operation to protect human rights between organisations such as the Council of Europe, the OSCE and the European Union (EU).[27] The Council of Europe Commissioner of Human Rights questioned whether the legal changes were consistent with the ECHR.[28]

Threat to free expression: legal restraints on journalism

Access to information and people's right to know

In order to combat corruption and to monitor public affairs, journalists need access to useful and reliable information. Despite a global flourishing of freedom of information over the past decade as dozens

---

26. See: www.newssafety.org and www.ifj.org for the reports of killings of journalists in Europe in 2010. The International News Safety Institute and its supporters, including the International Federation of Journalists and groups like Reporters Without Borders, regularly monitor and record the victims of violence in media and the failure of state authorities to bring the killers and those who ordered the killings to justice.
27. See: Resolution of the European Parliament (10 March 2011) on media law in Hungary, www.europarl.europa.eu/sides/getDoc.do?pubRef=-//EP//TEXT+TA+P7-TA-2011-0094+0+DOC+XML+V0//EN.
28. See: https://wcd.coe.int/wcd/ViewDoc.jsp?id=1751289&Site=CommDH&Back ColorInternet=FEC65B&BackColorIntranet=FEC65B&BackColorLogged=FFC679.

of countries have enacted laws guaranteeing people's right to know, the battle for open government has only been partly won.

Around 70 nations, covering more than half the world's population, have freedom-of-information laws. In Europe, the tradition of openness is a long one, stretching back to 1766 when Sweden established the right of citizens to ask for and receive any document from their rulers. But some countries in Europe do not uphold this tradition.

A 2006 survey by the Open Society Justice Initiative found some of Europe's new democracies in Armenia, Bulgaria and Romania significantly outperforming some older democracies in this area. The survey found particularly poor legislation in Austria, Spain and Italy.[29]

Some European countries have yet to act convincingly to rectify this and among those that have, new battles have to be fought to keep them on track. Often political and official institutions construct bureaucratic obstacles to transparency including heavy fees or a reduction in the number of staff available to deal with requests, leading to lengthy delays in providing requested information.[30]

At the same time, concerns about security and terrorism have led to a narrowing of available information with far more exceptions to what may be released. Such restrictions are spreading through international institutions such as the EU.

In 2008 the Council of Europe adopted the world's first treaty on access to information, the European Convention on Access to Official Documents, but this only applies to a narrow range of public bodies and, to the dismay of journalists, does not impose limits on the time taken to respond to requests.[31]

---

29. See: David Banisar (2006), "Freedom of information around the world 2006. A global survey of access to government information laws." www.privacyinternational. org/foi/foisurvey2006.pdf.
30. BBC World Service, "The Right to Know", 16 August 2008.
31. See: http://conventions.coe.int/Treaty/Commun/ListeTraites.asp?CM=8&CL =ENG.

Defamation

Equally troubling is governments' use of powerful defamation laws to punish legitimate journalism. These laws are often used to protect public figures from criticism even though human rights law requires people in public life to tolerate more scrutiny than ordinary people.

In Europe there is also the spectacle of celebrities and corporate leaders leaving their own countries to seek jurisdictions where their libel claims are more likely to succeed – so-called libel tourism. In March 2011 a grotesque example of this practice arose when a Ukrainian oligarch took his dispute with a Ukrainian newspaper about matters in the Ukraine to the British High Court.[32] He thought he could get a favourable verdict and generous compensation in a jurisdiction that provided media and journalists with less protection. Happily, the judge threw the case out but this sort of action shows how weak legislative protection of journalists, such as that in the United Kingdom, can have the effect of silencing legitimate journalism and investigative reporting in countries like the Ukraine.

The threat of prosecution has a deterrent effect on watchdog journalism, not just in the Ukraine, but across Europe. In 43 of the 56 participating states of the OSCE, journalists can go to prison for defamation.[33] Most western European countries retain criminal defamation on their statute books, even if the laws are rarely applied. In some countries previously under communist rule (Armenia, Bosnia and Herzegovina, Estonia, Georgia and Ukraine) such laws have been abolished, possibly because these countries have experience of how they were used to stifle dissent in their recent history.[34]

---

32. See: http://humanrightshouse.org/Articles/16005.html.
33. The 13 participating states in the OSCE region who, as per 11 July 2011, had fully decriminalised defamation are Armenia, Bosnia and Herzegovina, Cyprus, Estonia, Georgia, Kyrgyzstan, Moldova, Romania, Ireland, United Kingdom, Ukraine, Montenegro and the USA.
34. See: Regular Report to the Permanent Council of the OSCE by Dunja Mijatović, 16 December 2010.

According to figures from the Dutch Government, between January 2002 and June 2004 more than 100 people were incarcerated in the Netherlands for defamation, libel and insult. In 2005 five of the six freedom-of-expression cases decided by the Strasbourg Court involving western European states concerned defamation laws and the Court found a violation of free expression in four of the five. Journalists have also been sentenced for defamation in Belgium, Denmark, Malta, Finland, Italy, Norway and Switzerland. Since January 2005 at least 22 people in Europe and central Asia have been imprisoned for defamation.[35]

The OSCE Representative on Freedom of the Media has recommended that offences against "honour and dignity" be decriminalised and instead dealt with in civil law courts. The mere existence of criminal defamation laws could intimidate journalists and cause unfortunate self-censorship.

The Parliamentary Assembly of the Council of Europe has stated that "prison sentences for defamation should be abolished without further delay".[36] This decision was taken on the basis of a report which also suggested that public figures could not ask for more protection from defamation laws than ordinary citizens.[37]

The margin for criticism of politicians must in fact be broader, the Strasbourg Court has established. It has stated that politicians have to accept that their words and actions are open to a higher degree of scrutiny from both journalists and the public at large.[38]

Decriminalising defamation would not protect the media from civil law charges. This raises the problem of the very high damages being awarded in some cases. If the damages are not in proportion to the

---

35. See: www.article19.org/pages/en/defamation.html.
36. "Towards decriminalisation of defamation", Resolution 1577 (2007) http://assembly.coe.int/main.asp?Link=/documents/adoptedtext/ta07/eres1577.htm.
37. "Towards decriminalisation of defamation", Report by Committee on Legal Affairs and Human Rights, Doc. 11305, published on 25 June 2007, Rapporteur: Mr Jaume Bartumeu Cassany, Andorra, Socialist Group. http://assembly.coe.int/Main.asp?link=/Documents/WorkingDocs/Doc07/EDOC11305.htm.
38. *Lingens v. Austria*, Appl. No. 9815/82, judgment of 8 July 1986, paragraph 42.

actual injury, and if they are awarded against individual journalists, this again might have a "chilling effect".

Related to defamation, but not of the person, is the problem of insult laws and religion. For many journalists, blasphemy laws are particularly difficult to navigate, especially when they provide special protection for the core beliefs of a particular religion, but do not extend the same immunity to other beliefs, including ideas based upon a secular view of the world.

Blasphemy laws exist in most European countries (they have been repealed in Sweden and Spain) but application of the law is rare, and convictions are rarer still. In many countries where there was, or still is, a strong link between religion and the state, the law only protects one religion.

Threats to unwary journalists remain. In Ireland, for instance, an amendment to the country's Defamation Bill in 2009 provides for the offence of blasphemy if a person publishes material which is "grossly abusive or insulting to matters held sacred by any religion, thereby causing outrage among a substantial number of the adherents of that religion."

Right to privacy

Perhaps one of the most challenging tasks for journalists and human rights lawyers is to balance the competing rights of privacy and freedom of expression. Privacy and media freedom facilitate the enjoyment of other rights such as free expression, the right to act according to conscience and freedom of association.

Article 8 of the ECHR determines that every human being has a right to respect for private and family life and it has been called upon in many thousands of court cases, defending unfairly sacked employees, adulterers and victims of sexual harassment. However, in some countries, often where democratic traditions are weak, invasions of privacy routinely intersect with violations of other fundamental rights and freedoms including media freedom.[39]

---

39. A key global organisation campaigning for privacy is Privacy International. See: www.privacyinternational.org.

Although journalists understand well the need for privacy, they draw the line at confidentiality when it is used to limit accountability or to draw a curtain around hypocrisy and misconduct in public affairs.

It is of concern to the media when too rigorous application of privacy rules make it close to impossible for them to publish anything touching on the fundamental aspects of a person's private life such as their family life, sexual behaviour and orientation, or medical conditions, even where they believe that publication is in the public interest.

However, media concerns count for little when irresponsible journalists take liberties with the people they serve. The outrage in the United Kingdom that engulfed the global media network News Corporation over illegal phone hacking by its journalists, leading to the closure of one of Europe's best-selling newspapers, *News of the World*, provides a perfect illustration of how quickly reckless and intrusive journalism can damage public confidence.

The scandal was a devastating blow to Rupert Murdoch, the owner of News Corporation, who for decades has exercised powerful influence on political life in Britain. His ambitions to expand his company's ownership of the television market foundered dramatically in July 2011 amidst evidence that his newspapers had illegally hacked telephones, including that of a murdered teenager, and on other occasions bribed police for information. British parliamentarians, who have long lived in fear of his power, called on Murdoch and his son to appear before a parliamentary committee investigating the scandal. Advertisers withdrew their support. Share prices tumbled. The country's Press Complaints Commission (PCC) was humiliated and had to admit it had been deceived by the company.

For the first time in a generation the British press found itself at the heart of a crisis that centred on the unethical and illegal actions of journalists. Reporters, encouraged by circulation-hungry managers, had been hacking into private communications in the search for exclusive stories on the personal lives of the rich and famous. It was not only at *News of the World*. According to *The New York Times* other

British tabloids were also using the "dark arts" of hacking and "blagging" (deception and wilful misrepresentation) to get their stories.[40]

The reports of such behaviour were not new. In 2006 two men, including a *News of the World* reporter, were jailed for hacking into the telephones of members of the British royal family, but while the public may have turned a blind eye to journalists stalking the publicity-seeking celebrities of show business or sport, the mood changed suddenly when it was revealed by *The Guardian* that in 2002 the *News of the World* had hacked the telephone of 13-year-old murder victim Milly Dowler, giving her family false hope that their daughter was still alive. It emerged that other murder victims and family members of ordinary people killed by terrorist bombings may also have had their telephones hacked. The company's claims and solemn testimony to parliament and press regulators that the original phone hacking had been the work of "one rogue reporter" were exposed as fanciful. The predatory culture of intrusion that was uncovered caused widespread revulsion and led to an unprecedented backlash against irresponsible media management and unethical journalism, sparking a new and profound debate about regulation of the press.

Although phone hacking and a corrupt relationship between the Murdoch media and senior police officers which had helped cover up the story for years was only exposed thanks to some courageous journalism, particularly on the part of *The Guardian*, parliamentarians united in their demands for reform. The government announced a public inquiry into media conduct and for the first time in half a century the possibility of legal regulation of the press was thrust on to the policy agenda.

There are dangers in this. Public outrage is legitimate when the ethics of journalism are abandoned in pursuit of money and political influence, and when the press exercises power without responsibility, but it is no basis for curtailing media freedom.

---

40. Becker B. and Somaiya R. "In Court, Suggestions of Hacking Beyond The *News of the World*", *The New York Times*, 20 July 2011, www.nytimes.com/2011/07/21/world/europe/21london.html?_r=1&partner=rss&emc=rss.

Certainly, there is something to be said for curtailing the power of media oligarchies – of which News Corporation is a prime example – but that needs to be done in the name of pluralism, freedom and respect for privacy.

The Murdoch case, disgraceful though it is, should not be used as an excuse to impose heavy media regulation which would inhibit the capacity of investigative journalism. In most European countries good journalism plays a critical role in scrutiny of people in power. But good journalism is not the same as journalism that makes government or politicians happy. Indeed, it is the opposite.

In the United Kingdom, editors and journalists have been forced to recognise that public anger will not be easily quelled by assurances that ethical journalism can be trusted to balance respect for privacy with the media's need for legitimate investigation, scrutiny and disclosure. Journalists need to demonstrate more attachment to privacy rights. In all cases where privacy is in danger of violation, a journalist must consider the nature of someone's place in society, their reputation and their position in public life.

They must also be committed to transparency and fairness in their methods and they need to engage in new thinking about new forms of regulation that will restore public confidence and at the same time avoid the threat of political interference.

Such an approach could encourage states to exempt the media for acts of journalism which might otherwise be controversial, but which are carried out in the course of reporting where the organisation has committed to observe privacy standards. The key commitment must be, in the words of the code of conduct of the National Union of Journalists in the United Kingdom, to do nothing to intrude into anybody's private life, grief or distress unless justified by overriding consideration of the public interest.

Protection of sources in the context of state security

Although almost 100 countries, in one way or another, have recognised in law the right of journalists to protect people who provide them with information, there remains increasing pressure on reporters to reveal the names of whistle-blowers and confidential sources.

Governments in the United Kingdom, Germany, Italy, the Netherlands and Denmark, for instance, have been among those condemned for a range of offences, including tapping the telephones of journalists, planting spies in newsrooms, and prosecuting editors and reporters to gather information about journalists, their work and their sources.

Many of these incidents in recent years have arisen in the overheated atmosphere of counter-terrorism, under the cloak of security, raising fears that there is a weakening of civil liberties under way, particularly those of journalists.

Since the groundbreaking verdict of 1996 in the *Goodwin* case[41] when the Strasbourg Court ruled that, under Article 10, protection of sources was a right guaranteed in European human rights law, the Court has repeatedly reaffirmed the importance of this right. In a memorable phrase (in paragraph 39), the Court said that an order to disclose a source had a "potentially chilling effect" on the exercise of press freedom and continued:

> *Without such protection sources may be deterred from assisting the press in informing the public on matters of public interest. As a result the vital public-watchdog role of the press may be undermined and the ability of the press to provide accurate and reliable information may be adversely affected.*

The Court's recognition of this right is critical at a time when journalists are under pressure from police and the authorities to hand over computer files, photographs, film or notebooks, containing information about what they have witnessed or details of contacts.

When courts and public authorities ask journalists to hand over material or information that may reveal a source of information, most reporters will instinctively demur but occasions arise when journalists come to a different ethical conclusion and their conscience compels

---

41. *Goodwin v. the United Kingdom*, Appl. No. 17488/90, judgment of 27 March 1996.

them to co-operate with the authorities, as some did by giving evidence at the International Criminal Tribunal for the former Yugoslavia in The Hague.

Generally, the courts do not give reporters an absolute right to protect their sources and in recent years there have been numerous cases, some in the name of counter-terrorism, where the authorities have applied pressure, both open and covert, to obtain the names of those who gave confidential material to journalists.

Many journalists recognise the need in certain circumstances for exceptions to the principle of protection of sources, but they argue these should be applied in strictly controlled circumstances. In Belgium, for instance, the law provides that only a judge can decide to ask a journalist to disclose a source and then only when it is clear that:

- there is a serious threat to the physical integrity of the source;
- the information sought is crucial to prevent any harm to the physical integrity of people;
- the information required cannot be obtained by any other means.

Additionally, because freedom of expression is a human right, the courts may insist on a working definition of who is a journalist, if they are to have an exemption in law. If so, any definition of journalist must be as broad as possible. Journalists may be primary beneficiaries of legal protection of journalistic sources, but this protection should be extended to any person taking part in the journalistic process (including bloggers) where they show attachment to ethical principles.

Hate speech

The horrors of genocide and ethnic cleansing in Africa and the Balkans during the 1990s reveal just how ruthless politicians and unscrupulous academics, aided and abetted by willing journalists, can wage success-ful campaigns of hatred and violence based upon twisted theories of superiority.

However, sensationalist news reporting is not restricted to war and social conflict. Unprofessional and biased journalism in covering migration, religious freedom and intercultural relations in Europe can also do damage. At a time when economic and social uncertainty fuels anxiety in communities in many parts of Europe, some journalists are susceptible to manipulation by media-savvy political extremists who wish to foment racism and xenophobia.

The ethical dilemmas for journalists in this difficult climate bring into sharp relief the role of the media in confronting extremism and protecting vulnerable communities from bigotry and intolerance. But the tricky editorial judgments that journalists have to make are not helped when the battle against discrimination leads to the prohibition of speech or journalism just because it offends the sensitivities of one group or another. We have to guard against the use of the law to stifle criticism of people or beliefs.

Hate speech laws are a legitimate antidote to racism, incitement to hostility, discrimination or violence but in some countries these laws go beyond protection from objective harm and prohibit any statements which are perceived as offensive. Well intentioned though they are, laws such as those which forbid denial of historical truths or the wearing of offensive insignia may not be the most effective ways to combat racism and discrimination.

It can be argued that free expression and the application of ethical journalism can be part of a state's strategy for challenging prejudice, isolating extremists and promoting tolerance. Many journalists would say, for instance, that those who deny the Holocaust should be exposed to public ridicule rather than being imprisoned, as the history of this era is too well documented for it to be seriously questioned. Another problem with "denial laws" is their potential to proliferate. In October 2006, a draft law prohibiting denial of the 1915 Armenian genocide was adopted by the French National Assembly.

Although the Strasbourg Court famously concluded that free speech extends also to statements which "offend, shock or disturb",[42] some

---

42. *Handyside v. the United Kingdom*, Appl. No. 5493/72, judgment of 7 December 1976.

countries maintain laws that invite conflict between judges and journalists. In France, for instance, the *Loi sur la liberté de la presse* prohibits "attacks against honour" due to ethnicity, nationality, race or religion. This concern is well intentioned but such a provision can be misused to stifle criticism of a religious conviction or practice, even if that criticism is not motivated by hatred and is the expression of a sincerely held belief.

Meanwhile, Turkey prosecuted the writer Orhan Pamuk for "public denigration of Turkishness" on the basis of Article 301 of the Criminal Code after he referred to the killing of one million Armenians and 30 000 Kurds. The trial was halted in 2006 on technical grounds. Turkish journalist and writer Hrant Dink was convicted in 2005 for his statements in an article which concerned, *inter alia*, the issue of the Armenian genocide. He received threats from nationalists, who viewed him as a traitor, and he was murdered in January 2007. In September 2008 another Turkish writer, Temel Demirer, was charged under the same law after speaking out about Dink's murder.

This process is both ludicrous and dangerous. It raises the prospect of different states pursuing their own version of history by demanding that writers, journalists and all citizens keep to a script that is approved by the government. It opens the way to subjugating freedom of expression to nationalist agendas all over the world.

The Strasbourg Court has been careful to define a line between genuine incitement to violence and press freedom but in times of tension and public anxiety this is not certain. The Court ruled in October 2008, for instance, on a case against a French political cartoonist who was convicted in 2002 over a cartoon portraying the 11 September 2001 terrorist attack on the World Trade Center in New York. The caption parodied an advertising slogan: "We have all dreamed of it ... Hamas did it.*[sic]*"[43]

The drawing was published two days after the attack and, unsurprisingly, triggered a storm of protest. In its next issue, the magazine

---

43. See: Dirk Voorhoof, http://merlin.obs.coe.int/iris/2009/2/article1.en.html, on the judgment by the European Court of Human Rights (Fifth Section), case of *Leroy v. France*, Appl. No. 36109/03, 2 October 2008.

published reactions, including a contrite message from the cartoonist himself, who said his intention was not to add to the hurt of the victims, but only to communicate his own anti-Americanism.

By any standards the cartoon was insensitive, even gratuitously offensive, but as most journalists acknowledge, that is what cartooning is about. Nevertheless, the cartoonist and his publisher were found guilty of condoning terrorism under France's Press Act of 1881 and fined.

When the case was taken to Strasbourg, the Court rejected the appeal, finding that the cartoonist glorified the violent destruction of the United States of America, and diminished the dignity of the victims. They said his conviction by the French court was "necessary in a democratic society."

Journalists fear that judgments such as this may open the door to more prosecutions and convictions over media content that is regarded as offensive, rather than posing a serious and genuine threat to people and society.

Ethical journalism – the arguments

The persistent voice of journalism across Europe clamours for a media policy which supports ethical conduct and responsible use of information, but not for legal constraints.

However, to give their arguments more weight, media professionals must do more to put their own house in order. They need to isolate and expose those who betray the principles and standards of ethical journalism and they need to re-establish journalism as a force for dialogue, debate and democratic pluralism. To do that with conviction, journalists need to regulate their work in a credible manner.

Ethical reporting does not require a legal framework – although journalists who practise it do need the law to guarantee their rights to work freely – but to build credibility and public confidence journalism must adhere to codes of conduct and norms of ethical behaviour.

Codes of conduct

Most codes of conduct for journalists are aspirational and a statement of commitment from journalists to be responsible and accountable. In this way they provide protection for media owners and journalists from criticism and legal action.

There are more than 400 codes of one form or another in existence, most of which reflect a consistent set of common values and principles of journalism. Generally, these address accuracy and respect for the truth; impartiality and editorial independence; fair comment; respect for others; and correction of errors.[44]

Codes are the guarantor of value-based journalism and allegiance to a code is a benchmark for quality. They are also an important way of defining who is and who is not a journalist. Today that distinction is important not least because of the many new players in the world of information and the confusion over what rights they have in comparison to traditional journalists.

However, a code is only a starting point. Detailed guidelines and training are also needed to illustrate how ethical journalism works in practice. In this way good journalists are able, for example, to avoid hate speech, sexual stereotyping, or discrimination in reporting on minorities, and they have standards to follow when identifying and resolving conflicts of interest.

But even with sound codes and models of good practice to follow there can be no consistent body of ethical or quality journalism unless the principles of media freedom are defined in law, protected by the state and upheld in practice. Creating an ethical rights environment for journalism is, therefore, a duty of government as well as a responsibility of media practitioners.

---

44. The most extensive collection of available codes of conduct has been assembled by Media Accountability Systems and can be found at www.rjionline.org/mas/codes-of-ethics.php. A list of 50 codes in 30 European countries has been assembled by Ethicnet at http://ethicnet.uta.fi/. There is also a list developed in conjunction with the IFJ by The MediaWise Trust, www.mediawise.org.uk.

Self-regulation

Self-regulation is a solemn promise by quality-conscious journalists and media to correct their mistakes and to make themselves accountable. But for this promise to be fulfilled there must be two conditions: journalists and media have to behave ethically, and governments should not interfere in the media or use legal means to monitor and control the work of journalists.

For their part, across Europe, journalists' groups are mobilising around the notion of journalism as a public good, with programmes and campaigns recently launched in Germany, the United Kingdom, France, Russia, Italy and beyond. There is also fresh discussion about how to promote the responsible use of information, including the need for new guidelines and codes for bloggers and others.

Much of the debate, for instance in the United Kingdom in the wake of the phone hacking scandal, is on how to strengthen existing forms of media self-regulation to make them more relevant and credible.

In 2011, the weakness of the UK's PCC was exposed when it admitted that senior executives at Rupert Murdoch's *News of the World* had lied about the phone hacking affair. Though *The Guardian* had claimed that illegal phone hacking was widespread, the PCC twice investigated and dismissed these claims, accepting at face value *News of the World*'s assertion that "one rogue journalist" was responsible. The PCC even rebuked *The Guardian* when it reported fresh evidence of phone hacking, leading *The Guardian*'s editor to the resign from his position on the PCC.

In 2009 the European Federation of Journalists carried out its own investigation into the affair and issued a report which criticised the PCC for falling short of the standards expected of a self-regulating body. A committee of the British Parliament also criticised the PCC, saying its investigation into phone hacking was "simplistic, surprising, a further failure of self-regulation."[45]

---

45. "Press standards, privacy and libel", Report by Culture, Media and Sport Committee, Prepared 24 February 2010. See: www.publications.parliament.uk/pa/cm200910/cmselect/cmcumeds/362/36203.htm.

In early 2011, yet more revelations led to the arrest of journalists and executives at *News of the World*. Within weeks the paper had closed, its owner issued a public apology, a government inquiry was launched and the Chair of the PCC, Baroness Buscombe, resigned.

Although there is little appetite for state regulation of the media across the British press and the political class, a debate has been launched which will almost certainly lead to a robust new structure for monitoring the press. The principle of self-regulation may survive, but there are compelling arguments for change and to give any new authority extra powers to investigate the press and enforce its judgments.

This review comes at a time when it is increasingly clear across Europe that many structures for monitoring and judging media content are hardly fit for purpose in the multimedia age. The days when press and television media content can be sensibly divided into separate and viable jurisdictions, one relying on the goodwill of press owners, the other, part of a state administration underpinned by law, may be coming to a close.

Today information often appears in a single stream of content available simultaneously on different platforms – video, audio, online and printed text. News and information flows from a converged multimedia environment, but much of it is regulated by laws and structures from a bygone age.

Reworking notions of media accountability invites a new vision of media regulation, one which goes beyond bureaucratic frameworks for policing journalism, and which encourages self-regulation as a positive force for setting high standards and defending them. This may be achieved by adapting existing press councils or state media commissions, but less complex forms of peer review will continue, such as the use of readers' editors or ombudsmen, or through professional journals and the systematic monitoring and reporting on media by NGOs and human rights bodies.

New systems may benefit from legal guarantees, but unless they are cast in the mould of self-rule and provide an independent voice for civil society, they will constantly face the danger of undue political or corporate influence.

One key question is that of funding. Who pays for media accountability? In some countries, such as Germany and Sweden, taxpayers do pay some of the costs, but the media also pay their share. Any budgetary support from the state for self-regulation must be provided according to principles which ensure transparency and accountability, and which provide safeguards against governmental or political interference.

Media accountability, in whatever form it comes, must balance the rights of the individual and the community, and the rights of journalists and the press. But it must not be self-serving. It is vital that press councils act on behalf of the public and the profession and are not, as with the PCC in the United Kingdom, perceived to be there to shield media owners from criticism or ethical scrutiny. Effective self-regulation must include rules for transparency on political affiliation and ownership of media.

Journalism itself is a necessary part of the means by which power is held to account, but on its own, even with the best architecture for self-regulation, it is not enough. The fabric of accountability also requires an independent judiciary and trustworthy lawmakers as well as statutory watchdogs, auditors, ombudsmen and privacy authorities, all able to play a role in making society transparent and sensitive to rights.

Many press councils and media commissions are set up by the media themselves. But to build public confidence they must provide a set of credible rules under which people featured in the news media can complain if something is inaccurate, intrusive or unfair. In short, a media accountability system needs to:

- mediate complaints from the public in a transparent service, free of charge, and provide remedies for unethical conduct by journalists;
- help build trust between journalists and the public to ensure that the media can resist political and economic pressure;
- protect journalistic independence and media freedom in society;
- ensure the right of the public to be informed;
- support social and professional conditions that will enable journalists to serve their public better;

- foster better understanding within society at all levels about the role played by independent journalism in democratic life;
- support journalists in their work and encourage professional solidarity.

This is not a manifesto for policing. It is about mediation, advocacy and education, and seeking opportunities for fresh dialogue within society about the media and the need to support ethical journalism.

Building support for rights and ethics

Building the professional base of European journalism is a constant, permanent process. There are a number of current initiatives and activities that give a practical dimension to a new debate about ethical behaviour in journalism and the role of media in rights protection.

Ethical Journalism Initiative (EJI)

Launched by the International Federation of Journalists in 2005, this extensive programme of support for training in ethical journalism and debate about the future of journalism has been launched across the Middle East and Asia. In 2010, country-specific programmes were established in Azerbaijan and Russia.[46]

In 2011, a European EJI programme for Lithuania, Slovakia and Greece was launched in co-operation with ARTICLE 19 and the Media Diversity Institute. Studies are being prepared on ethical reporting of defamation of religion, migration and diversity. An EJI study and report on self-regulation and media accountability will be published in 2011, covering all major European countries.

European standards of media ethics

In 2011, following a two-year project, the United Nations Educational, Scientific and Cultural Organization published a book examining media self-regulation in south-eastern Europe and Turkey. Involved

---

46. See: www.ethicaljournalisminitiative.org.

were the OSCE, the Alliance of Independent Press Councils of Europe and the South East European Network for Professionalization of Media.[47]

Charter of Rome

Italian publishers and journalists issued an industry code of conduct in 2008 to promote ethical reporting of refugee and immigration issues. This initiative followed protests by the United Nations High Commission for Refugees over racist media coverage of a multiple murder. The code sets out ethical guidelines and is part of a programme that includes awareness raising, training and the creation of an independent observatory monitoring media coverage of discrimination.[48]

Media4Diversity

A 30-country study on media and diversity in EU member states and Iceland, Norway and Liechtenstein was published in 2009. It provided specific examples of good professional practice and aimed at improving quality of journalism in reporting on issues of discrimination.[49]

Camden Principles

Human rights groups and media supporters are seeking endorsement for the Camden Principles on Freedom of Expression and Equality, adopted in 2009. The Camden Principles represent a progressive interpretation of international law and standards and were compiled by a high-level group of policymakers, academics and experts in humanitarian rights law, journalism and public affairs.[50]

---

47. UNESCO (2011), *Professional journalism and self-regulation: New media, old dilemmas in South East Europe and Turkey*, UNESCO, Paris.
48. The Code of Conduct is a protocol to the Charter of Duties of Journalists (La Carta dei doveri del giornalista).
49. European Commission (2009), *Media4Diversity: Taking the pulse of diversity in the media*, Office for Official Publications of the European Communities, Luxembourg. Prepared by IFJ, Internews Europe and the Media Diversity Institute.
50. Published April 2009 by ARTICLE 19.

Conclusions

In redefining ethical journalism as a public good, we introduce a new narrative about the importance of ethical information and how European society is informed. In this sense the revival of the notion of mission in journalism is to be encouraged. But successful revival will not happen automatically. In order to rekindle a sense of mission and commitment to core principles of journalism it is necessary to improve the conditions – social, professional and legal – in which journalists work.

Many journalists already work in precarious conditions and they often find themselves further constrained by laws which weaken protection of sources or restrict scrutiny of public figures and government.

Particularly in times of concern over security and terrorism, there is a need to protect the rights of people to be properly informed against the imposition of rules that may be intended to protect communities, but can be used to reinforce secrecy and undermine civil liberties.

Journalists and the media seek a liberating environment, buttressed by media policy that nourishes transparency, encourages professional training, ethical conduct and self-regulation, and promotes innovation and fresh thinking about the future of the media.

Although the Internet and social networks bring the audience into play as never before and encourage more information activism, this is not a substitute for ethical journalism which respects the rights of others. Democracy and pluralism require information professionals with skills and competence, and whose work is shaped by a framework of values.

The information challenge, therefore, is not just about journalism or the people who work in the media. It concerns new dialogues within journalism and involving media practitioners, civil society and policy-makers to promote new forms of discourse and humanitarian values in all sections of society.

In this work governments have a key role to play. Reform and renewal of the public information space require fresh thinking on media policy.

Many governments will be cautious, certainly after the experience of Hungary in 2010 and its controversial reform of media law, but some general principles for media policy can be suggested. Governments should:

- provide constitutional support for freedom of expression with narrowly defined limits reflected in law;
- review legislation affecting the media and journalism, and repeal outdated and unused statutes that have the potential to intimidate, silence or otherwise stifle legitimate expression in the public interest;
- enact viable and useful rules on access to information from public bodies, with limited and narrowly defined exceptions;
- decriminalise defamation and avoid punitive fines in civil cases;
- review funding and technical assistance programmes for media to support pluralism and diversity, and structures for self-regulation, but do so without compromising editorial independence; and
- strengthen and update systems of media accountability and reinforce principles of self-regulation in an integrated and open media environment.

In all of this the aim is to create a modern vision of journalism, one that suits the age. Such a vision would revive the notion of mission in journalism, and appeal to idealism and dedication to principles that nourish democracy and respect for human rights, not just in the media but across the whole of society.

Chapter 3:
Access to official documents

Anders R. Olsson, journalist, author and expert on transparency and public access to information

> Open government promotes fair and equal treatment under the law and efficiency in public administration – and it strengthens democracy.

Summary

Open government is a prerequisite for a functioning democracy. Transparency promotes fair and equal treatment under the law and efficiency in public administration. In order to achieve this, citizens – very often journalists – must be able to find the documents they need to see.

The aim of this chapter is to study how open government can be promoted. Sweden is used as an example: in this country citizens' right to access official documents has been constitutionally guaranteed for more than 200 years. It is considered an important element of the right to free speech. If citizens lack access to reliable and relevant information about their society, free speech will be of limited value to them.

Access rights have traditionally been extended as far as possible, with limitations put in place only at the level where the work of public officials might otherwise be seriously hampered. However, this tendency to maximise transparency has been met, beginning some 30 years ago, with waves of criticism. As a result, citizen access to electronically stored information has gradually been restricted.

The Swedish model for openness must be understood as a system, a regime based on the understanding that rules on citizens' access to documents are no more than a first step towards creating transparency. This initial step needs to be complemented by other laws and administrative regulations to have the desired effect. In Sweden, the right of public officials – on their own initiative and without penalties – to inform journalists is legally protected. How the authorities register and handle documents is regulated. The administrative courts and the institution of the Parliamentary Ombudsman have important functions in the defence of citizens' right to access information within the public sector.

Although the political tradition of openness is strong and the societal effects of the model are generally encouraging, the future of the Swedish model is not necessarily bright. Conflicts about privacy protection and international pressure on the legislature to "harmonise"

Swedish law with the legal regimes of European Union (EU) members less oriented towards transparency have for several years created friction and heated debate within Sweden and will continue to do so.

Introduction

For about 15 years, "transparency" has been a political buzzword at the international level. In 2007, it was reported that more than 70 countries had or were developing major disclosure policies or laws.[51] The reach and the strength of these laws vary considerably, but they are clearly a sign of a political trend. In 2009, the Council of Europe adopted a Convention on Access to Official Documents.[52] In its preamble, the arguments for transparency are eloquently summarised. No doubt today, the need for openness is generally recognised.

Most of this legislation focuses on the public sector, although the need for transparency is apparent in the private sector as well. In the aftermath of corporate scandals such as at Enron, Worldcom and the Murdoch media empire, demands for greater transparency in the private sector are becoming increasingly vociferous. So far though, little has happened regarding "openness" in financial institutions or other multinational corporations. In a market economy the obstacles to realising transparency within private, competing companies appear huge. Creating transparency in public institutions is, at least in the near future, a more realistic option.

The Swedish experience

To assess the long-term effects of transparency reform, the Swedish experience can serve as a frame of reference. The country's law on citizen access to official documents is very old, first introduced in 1766 as part of a Freedom of the Press Act. This act made Sweden the first country in the world to grant constitutional protection for free

---

51. Florini A. (ed.) (2007), *The right to know. Transparency for an open world*. Columbia University Press, New York.
52. See: http://conventions.coe.int/Treaty/EN/Treaties/Word/205.doc.

speech.[53] Access rights and free speech guarantees were abolished a few years later, but were reintroduced in 1810 and have remained in force ever since.

Today, Swedish laws that aim to create transparency are commonly referred to as: *offentlighetsprincipen*. The word "Offentlighet" could in some contexts be translated into "openness", but let us use the "transparency-principle" as a practical, although not literal translation.[54] The principle is manifested in several ways in Swedish law and is not quite translatable. It applies to the public sector as a whole.

It is important to note that Swedish rights to access have never been specified as rights for media professionals – they are for everyone. Chapter two of the act begins: "In order to encourage the free interchange of opinion and the enlightenment of the public, every Swedish subject shall have free access to official documents."

A practical example

Before discussing the societal effects of this historically unique reform, let us describe it by following a person, living in Sweden, who searches for publicly held information. We will assume that she is a woman and we will call her X.

The basic principle is that when X turns to a state or municipal agency and asks to see an "official document", it should be handed over immediately and at no cost.[55] A "document" is defined here as a presentation in writing or images but also a recording that one can read, listen to or comprehend only with the use of technical equipment. The word "document" consequently refers not only to hard copy writing or

---

53. The reasons Sweden adopted such radical legislation as early as the 18th century are somewhat contested among historians, but at the time, of course, ordinary people were not expected to speak publicly or seek to access official documents. The rights for "all" were conceived as rights for the elite.
54. The alternative would be "Freedom of Information Principle", but this expression is further from the Swedish term.
55. There are of course limitations, some pertaining to secrecy statutes. See below for further details.

images, but also information stored on other media, for example a magnetic tape or a computer hard disk. Simply put, a document is an object containing information. An "official document" is something that is actually available to the agency, and given its final form. It can be either drawn up by the authority or sent to it.

The Freedom of the Press Act contains many rules specifying when a document is considered to have been finalised – drawn up – by a public authority. Thus, it becomes official as soon as the authority dispatches it. A document which is not dispatched is considered drawn up when the matter to which it relates is finally settled by the authority. If the document is not related to a specific matter, it is drawn up when it has been finally checked or has otherwise received its final form. A diary, a journal or similar document that is enlarged on a continuing basis is considered to be drawn up as soon as it is ready to be used.

Falling outside the definition of an official document is, for example, a draft of a decision or a written internal communication in a matter as long as no final determination has been made.

Documents sent to the agency become official as soon as they reach the mailbox (real or virtual) of the agency or otherwise become available to someone working for it. Even a message not addressed to the public authority but to the home of one of its officers becomes official – if it relates to the authority's activities – as soon as it is delivered. The document need not be registered anywhere in order to reach the legal status of "official".

It is irrelevant whether or not the documents that X now wants to see personally concern her. The agency, under normal circumstances, is not allowed to ask for the identity of X nor the reasons for her interest in the documents. The fact that citizens do not have to identify themselves means that foreigners also have access to government-held information.

Secrecy: limits to public access to information

For obvious reasons, the legislation on citizens' access to documents does not mean absolute transparency. According to chapter two of the Freedom of the Press Act, the *Riksdag* (Parliament) is allowed to pass legislation limiting public access to information in seven areas, including that related to:

- security of the realm or its relations with a foreign state or an international organisation;
- central financial, monetary or foreign exchange policy of the realm;
- inspection, control or other supervisory activities of a public authority;
- preventing or prosecuting crime;
- public economic interests;
- protection of the personal integrity or economic circumstances of private subjects; or
- preservation of animal or plant species.

Content of official documents may not be kept secret in order to protect interests other than those listed above. Exactly what kind of information shall be kept secret is stated in basic law in the Openness and Secrecy Act (OSA). The government may not decide on the limits of secrecy, this is an exclusive right of the *Riksdag*. However, in a number of provisions of the OSA, the government is allowed to make supplementary regulations. These regulations are stipulated in a Secrecy Ordinance.

The OSA has several hundred clauses on secrecy, but the act also has a number of provisions describing how the authorities should answer requests and their duty to inform an applicant of the right to appeal. It also contains important regulations on how public documents must be registered.

A right to access documents is the rule. The authorities can deny citizens access only under provisions specified in law.

How to gain access

To gain access, X approaches a state agency that holds information of interest to her. The agency must provide access while it is operative. For a typical administrative authority that would be during office hours, say between 9 a.m. and 7 p.m. on weekdays. In a police station manned day and night however, citizens can have access to documents at any time.

In order to obtain the relevant official documents X must be able to describe them, in reasonably clear terms. The description need not be precise. It is not necessary for X to be able to state dates or registration numbers. On the other hand, the authorities are not liable to make extensive inquiries in order to find relevant documents when the applicant is unable to provide enough detail.

A request to obtain an official document shall be dealt with speedily by the authority. The exact wording in the key clause of the Freedom of the Press Act is "made available … forthwith, or as soon as possible". Thus, a civil servant receiving X's request to see documents is obliged to treat it as his or her top priority.

There are of course situations where providing a document can take time. One reason may be that the authority must consider whether some of the information contained in the document is secret or not, according to the OSA. If the request is for hundreds or even thousands of documents, examination of the material may require several hours or days of work.

Information cannot be classified as secret beforehand. A formal decision must be taken, whenever access to the contents of a document is asked for and refused. Anybody refused access to an official document is entitled to a written statement, referring to the statute that the decision is based upon, and must be informed about the right to appeal. An appeal shall be dealt with promptly.

If the document that X is asking for cannot be made available, in the agency's opinion, without the disclosure of classified information, she may respond in one of three ways. She can:
- appeal against the decision, following which the matter will be tried in an administrative court;[56]

---

56. The applicant does not need a lawyer to make the appeal, and it is free of charge.

- choose to explain what she intends to do with the classified information, in the hope of convincing the agency that no harm will be done by providing access. The agency can then – but is under no compulsion to – allow her to see the document subject to reservations restricting her rights to use the information covered by an OSA paragraph. The applicant may, for example, be forbidden to publish the information or to use it for purposes other than research; or

- accept the agency's interpretation of the OSA and be content with having the rest of the document, the non-secret parts, made available in the form of a transcript or copy.

If the documents to which X is given access cannot be read or comprehended without the use of technical aids, the authority must make such equipment available – for example a computer or a tape recorder.

When given access, X may read or examine the documents on the spot. She can also transcribe, photograph or record them. On request, the agency must provide a copy of the document for her. Copies are free of charge up to nine pages. For 10 pages or more, the agency can charge X a fee covering the costs of copying.

Supervision

Administrative courts are important to safeguard citizens' right to access official documents, as is the institution of the Parliamentary Ombudsman. The four Parliamentary Ombudsmen spend considerable time and effort dealing with complaints regarding access issues. A common reason for complaints is that agencies do not answer requests quickly enough.

Most Swedes never take advantage of their right to see official documents. They may be aware of the legislation, but cannot describe it in sufficient detail and rarely find themselves in situations where they need this kind of information. Journalists and researchers, as well as politically, commercially or socially active persons, are those who most make use of their access rights. Typically, government and municipal agencies, dealing with issues of interest to news reporters, are kept "on their toes" because persons frequently demand access to their documents. Agencies of less interest for the mass media – the majority – tend to get less training and make more mistakes when approached by citizens asking to see documents.

Additional legislation on transparency

To understand how the Swedish law on access contributes to a healthier democracy – an issue to be discussed below – it must be put into context. The protection of journalists' sources, for example, is an important part of the system to ensure transparency.

In Sweden, as in all comparable states, there are massive numbers of documents in the public sector. The databases are numerous and some of them contain enormous amounts of data. If there is information there suggesting foul play of some kind, journalists almost always need help to find it. And finding it is not always enough. The information may well be complicated; it may take legal, technical or economic expertise to understand it.

The experts are usually not difficult to find, but will they help? Will they point the journalist to the publicly held information that – assembled and explained – makes it possible for him or her to start a serious investigation? This depends on the circumstances.

Protection of sources is crucial. Swedish law – and we are still within constitutional law – states that if someone approaches a journalist, and offers to provide information anonymously, the journalist has a strict obligation to protect the identity of this source. Revealing the name of such an informant can result in the journalist being sentenced to up to 12 months in jail.[57]

---

57. The journalist may have to tell an editor in charge where the information came from because the editor will be legally responsible for publishing the story. But if told the identity of the source, the editor is bound by the same legal framework of professional secrecy as the reporter.

What if this human source is bound by his or her own rules of professional secrecy? In the public sector, the OSA applies. The OSA clarifies what civil servants can and cannot tell a reporter. Regarding the most sensitive information, the statutes demand absolute secrecy, and in doing so define the other statutes as demanding a secrecy less than total. Most paragraphs in the OSA actually allow civil servants to verbally present classified information to a reporter. They are not allowed to hand over a document with the classified information, but they can, if they see fit, read the document to the reporter. This rather strange legal solution (apparently, no other country has anything similar) goes to show how serious Swedish legislators have been in their efforts to create an open society.

It is also important to point out that when a civil servant anonymously exercises his or her right to inform a reporter, it is expressly forbidden for other civil servants to try and find out who "leaked" the information. The constitutionally protected right to inform journalists anonymously about almost everything was described a hundred years ago by a governmental commission as "the safety valve which alone makes it possible in many a case for words to be spoken that ought to be spoken, for facts to be brought forward that ought be brought forward".

Strong protection for media sources is not without complications. Public officials entrusted with secret information of value to the mass media are often willing, especially when offered financial reward, to tip off journalists. The line between making use of the right to free speech and corrupt behaviour is not easily drawn here. In Sweden, the fact that police officers often anonymously leak information to journalists has caused the most controversy. It has been argued that such leaks occasionally are detrimental to police investigations, and demands for a tighter secrecy regime in the police force have been raised repeatedly. So far though, the "safety valve" has been left open for police officers.

Strong protection for media sources is just one of several components necessary to maintain real transparency in the public sector. Transparency cannot be realised with just a few clauses on citizen access to documents;

it must be seen as a quality within a system requiring legal support from many angles and on several levels. When discussing whether the Swedish transparency model works as well in practice as claimed by its most enthusiastic supporters, a few other components should be mentioned. Before that, however, a few words on legal developments and the political debate concerning the Swedish level of openness.

Transparency versus privacy protection

Although the value of the principle of transparency is uncontested in Sweden, the level of openness is constantly under debate. Some argue that so many exceptions to the principle have been introduced during the last 30 years that, in 2011, Swedish claims to having an open society are unjustified. Undoubtedly, many exceptions have been added. Most, though not all, target information held by the authorities in electronic form. Thirty years ago, virtually any information that could be extracted from a computer file or a database fell under the definition of "official document". This is no longer so. Citizen access to electronically stored information is nowadays quite limited.

At least as common, however, is the argument that Sweden's transparency model constitutes a threat to the privacy of citizens. Several hundred clauses of the OSA protect personal data, but even so the amount of information about individuals still available in official documents is substantial. Thus it is argued that the strong emphasis on transparency in the public sector has an unacceptable side effect – the underdeveloped protection of the individual.

This debate is ongoing and fuelled by both technological and political developments. To the dismay of most privacy advocates, a surprisingly large part of the population is willing to share a lot of personal information with anyone – using Facebook and other social forums. On the political level though, privacy advocates still seem to have the upper hand, at least in part because Swedish legal standards on free speech and access to official documents are under pressure.

The EU demands harmonisation. Considering how small (in terms of population) Sweden is – and how few of the other members support radical access legislation – it seems likely that European norms on privacy protection will win out and Swedish ideals of transparency will be suppressed accordingly.

In a verdict drawing some attention, the European Court of Human Rights came to the conclusion that German law should not have allowed magazines like *Bunte* and *Freizeit Revue* to publish pictures of Princess Caroline of Monaco taken when she was appearing in public places: riding, shopping, eating at a restaurant. There was nothing offensive in the pictures, but the Court still maintained that their publication breached her right to protection of private life, guaranteed in Article 8 of the European Convention on Human Rights.[58]

To publish pictures such as these would not have been considered illegal in Sweden, and the country has no law granting general protection for privacy. There is an obvious risk that Swedish legislation also would fail, in the eyes of the Court, to meet the demands of Article 8. Although it could be argued that the Court's verdicts on privacy issues are not altogether consistent, its approach is quite troubling to advocates of the Swedish tradition of free speech and transparency.

The value and the downside of transparency can and will be discussed as long as our countries are governed democratically. Although not the only relevant one, the single most important issue in this regard is – and will most likely remain – privacy protection. Why then, has Sweden come to approach the conflict between transparency and privacy protection differently from most other countries? Let us take a closer look.

There are several common arguments for open government. Information held by the authorities is there in the public interest and should therefore be available to everyone. Transparency is important to guarantee the accountability of the authorities at all levels, promoting citizens' trust. Institutions of power which are better informed are able to exploit and abuse less informed citizens. Regimes of secrecy tend to breed arbitrariness, inefficiency and corruption.

---

58. *Von Hannover v. Germany*, Appl. No. 59320/00, judgment of 24 June 2004.

These are good arguments. The traditional Swedish approach to explaining the value – some might say necessity – of transparency in the public sector is divided into three arguments. The second and third arguments are in accordance with those already mentioned. The second concerns efficiency: dysfunctional institutions will attract attention sooner if they work "on stage" than they would working behind closed doors. The third is about democracy. Authorities at all levels, both government agencies and local authorities, need to gather information about the society they serve. If as much of that information as possible is also available to citizens, the quality of debate on societal issues will be higher. Democracy needs well-informed citizens.

The first argument, however, directly addresses the conflict between openness and privacy protection. It refers to the rule of law. Open government is a way of ensuring that citizens are treated fairly and equally – and in accordance with the law. Citizens who suspect that they are not treated correctly should have the right to see for themselves how others are treated. If citizen A is not allowed to build a tool shed in his garden, but his neighbour B is, A needs to see B's application and the formal decision from the local authority; otherwise A will not be able to find out if building permits are granted equally and fairly. Therefore personal data in documents held by the authorities should be publicly available unless there are obvious reasons for keeping it secret.

If it is reasonable to believe that the content of a document could cause economic, physical or psychological harm to an individual if it were made publicly available, a rule of secrecy could apply. Secrecy then, would typically cover information indicating something about a person's physical or mental health, political convictions, religious beliefs, sexual orientation or alcohol or drug use. The basic idea, though, is to have a "two-step test". The first step would ask if it is likely that a specific piece of personal information, if publicly available, would cause harm to the individual. If the answer is yes, the second step would ask: is citizens' access to this kind of information clearly of greater importance than the protection of the individual?

It is worth mentioning that the right of X to access a certain document does not automatically give her the right to publish the content. Personal data in a police investigation may be accessible in a police station or a court of law, but dissemination could well constitute libel. A newspaper editor can be found guilty of libel if the paper has described a person in a way that is likely to expose him or her to the contempt of others. This is the basic rule, which means that truth is not an absolute defence.

The Swedish approach to access rights should be compared to the way most democracies have chosen transparency as a guiding principle for their courts of law. Court proceedings in European (and many other) countries are normally open to citizens and written verdicts are publicly available. This means that much personal information about individuals on trial for criminal behaviour will be exposed. Not only that, victims of crime and even witnesses may have to reveal sensitive information in this public arena. Maintaining trust in the court system is usually considered more important in this conflict of interests.

The difference between Sweden and most other democracies is that Sweden applies the same argument to the public sector as a whole. All authorities make decisions of importance to citizens, at the very least about how to make use of taxpayers' money, and in some instances decisions as important as verdicts from a court of law. Transparency should be the rule, and secrecy – when necessary to avoid harm – the exception.

With the rise of the ideology of general data protection, however, the Swedish model based on evaluating the sensitivity of personal data has been severely undermined. The concept of data protection, developed in the 1970s, is based on the assumption that all handling and dissemination of personal data must be minimised, in order to promote privacy protection on a societal level. Harm-testing thus becomes irrelevant, since danger stems from personal data as such: the more personal information – sensitive or not – available for gathering and analysis, the more certain it is that invasions of privacy will occur.[59]

---

59. This leads to questions about the possibility of extracting sensitive information out of larger quantities of non-sensitive personal data – issues of "data mining" and "profiling". They are complex and will not be explored here.

It must be stressed that access rights that completely exempt personal data become very limited in reach. Authorities making decisions about individuals, as well as for social planning and the allocation of societal resources, do so using personal data. These decisions, often crucial to citizens, cannot be critically monitored by an outsider without access to the basic data upon which they are based. In the conflict between access rights and policies of data protection, a great deal of transparency is at stake.

The arguments for general data protection may not have won every Swede over but, as already indicated, Swedish politicians have in recent years found themselves caught between two competing interests. The national tradition of transparency is so strong that it cannot, at least not openly, be questioned. On the other hand, external pressure has been mounting to adopt general data-protection policies. As noted above, the *Riksdag* has, without much public debate, taken a number of steps to limit citizen access to electronically stored information, usually referring to the need for privacy protection. This may have reduced the tension between Swedish ideals of openness and typically European ideals of data protection, but it has not been eliminated.

Weighing the arguments for transparency against the arguments for privacy protection is indeed a complex task.

One reason for this is that the value of transparency is so difficult to elucidate. This has created an imbalance. The price people pay for openness is usually made public, whereas the price paid for secrecy is not. When access to official documents actually creates a situation where someone is being harmed – and the harm could have been avoided with more secrecy – it is often reported by journalists and made widely known. An example could be a doctor or a teacher reported to a supervisory authority for serious professional misconduct, perhaps serious enough to attract the attention of journalists. The accusations may later turn out to be unsubstantiated but impossible to prove false. The damage done to a reputation could well be irreparable.

These situations are rare, but do occur – and are probably unavoidable with any access legislation that has teeth. There is an obvious public interest in the reporting of professional misconduct in many areas. When it happens, there is an identified victim and people engaging in his or her cause. Even politicians who really support the idea of open government will then find it difficult to reject demands for more secrecy.

Transparency advocates, on the other hand, can never point to the victims of secrecy. They remain unknown. When information that citizens really need to have in order to act in their own interest is successfully withheld, no one will know. No one will protest. No demands for more transparency will be heard. Thus secrecy has a tendency to spread, slowly and almost irresistibly, to cover more and more information in the hands of the authorities.[60]

European Union transparency policies

The EU has battled internally about the appropriate level of openness for at least 15 years. An important step was taken in 2001 when it adopted Regulation No. 1049/2001 regarding Public Access to European Parliament, Council and Commission Documents, giving citizens a right to access documents at those EU institutions. The regulation shares several of the virtues of the Swedish legislation, but there are a few important differences. The secrecy requirements are described only in general terms, making it difficult for citizens to argue their case when denied access to information. Personal data is not subject to sensitivity-testing and is normally considered classified. Another difference is that EU institutions are granted more time (up to three weeks) to answer requests from citizens.

A tug-of-war between member states, civil society, the European Commission and the European Parliament on openness has been under way since the regulation was introduced. Conflicts have arisen about which documents the regulation should cover, the levels of secrecy, the right of a member country sending documents to an EU institution to influence decisions on their accessibility, and many other topics.

---

60. A study conducted in 2002 of how the number of clauses on secrecy in Swedish law increases year by year is available in Swedish at: www.sjf.se.

To summarise developments, it seems that the EU in 2011 is taking steps towards less, not more transparency. A few recent verdicts – all from 2010 – from the European Court of Justice illustrate this trend. In both *Commission v. Technische Glaswerke Ilmenau* (C-139/07 P) and *Sweden/API/Commission* (C-514/07 P, C-528/07 P, C-532/07 P) the European Court of Justice actually changed the presumption of openness, established previously in its case law, to a presumption of secrecy. This is not just a question of how to describe the glass – half-full or half-empty. When secrecy becomes the rule and access to information the exception this needs to be justified, as it is a decisive shift of power. If citizens should be required to explain their reasons for accessing official documents, and the authorities and courts must decide on the cogency of their arguments, this is a significant step away from the transparency-principle.

It remains to be seen if the European Court of Justice will interpret the regulation on access rights in the same way in future cases, but it is obvious that case law fluctuates on this issue. Less transparency will most likely be the result.

When asked about the extent to which the national Swedish legislation on transparency is affected by EU decisions and policies, leading Swedish politicians generally claim that no such influences exist. In fact, both at the beginning of negotiations about membership and at their conclusion in 1994, the Swedish delegation declared – officially but one-sidedly – that the transparency-principle and citizens' constitutionally protected right to inform journalists were fundamental parts of the national political heritage and would not be affected by EU membership.

Since then, the *Riksdag* has limited access rights in a number of ways, in particular access to electronically stored information, but no such decisions have been taken with reference to what the EU might like or dislike. One example is the (estimated) 150 new laws on specific state databases, strictly limiting citizens' right to access information from larger collections of personal data at government agencies.[61] Most neutral observers agree that the *Riksdag*, feeling the pressure from "data-protection oriented" European courts, is trying hard to adjust, although very discreetly, to a mainstream EU position on transparency.

Societal effects of transparency

The question Swedes are always asked about their national model of transparency is: does it really work?

There are at least three answers to this question, depending on what is meant by "work": Yes, Yes and No. To explain, let us repeat the three different arguments traditionally referred to in defence of Swedish access laws. Citizens' right to access promotes fair and equal treatment under the law, as well as efficiency and democracy. I find that the Swedish experience proves that all these arguments are valid. Of course, citizen access to official documents does not guarantee any of these qualities in a society, but without access rights it is far more difficult to establish them.

The first Yes relates to the civil servants themselves. The elites within politics and major bureaucracies are not really enthusiastic about transparency. Publicly, they always stress the value of open government and access legislation, and when speaking generally about our political culture they are probably honest. However, when something goes wrong within their organisation and journalists begin to investigate, their appreciation of Swedish access legislation turns out to be quite limited. The many steps to effectively minimise citizen access to electronically stored information – the first taken more than 30 years ago – also illustrate how legislators as pragmatists tend to be less supportive of access rights than they are as theorists.

For precisely the same reason that legislators and bureaucratic elites can have doubts about the value of openness, low and middle-level

---

61. These laws not only curb citizen access to the personal data as such – to a large extent classified anyway, under the OSA – but also to statistical information based on the content of these databases.

civil servants appreciate effective access legislation. It becomes a safety guarantee for them. As long as they have done what they have been ordered to do, they are safe. Responsibility for the failure of an authority, whatever it is, lands where it should land – on the desks of the leaders. With a non-transparent administration, those in charge are more easily able to avoid responsibility. They can blame others, they can delay investigations or at least create so much confusion that accountability is more difficult to achieve.

The second Yes is about revealing weaknesses and misbehaviour in the public sector. It is true for Sweden and probably for most countries that civil servants usually want to do, and really try to do, a good job. Nevertheless, occasionally things go wrong. It could be due to their own incompetence or even laziness, but difficulties could just as well be caused by circumstances beyond their control. They could stem from ill-informed or unrealistic orders from the political level. It could simply be a matter of bad luck, with trouble that no one could anticipate.

We can disregard the reasons. Something goes wrong in the middle of a project or some administrative process. Only then may civil servants feel the urge to cover something up. With strict laws on open government in place, this is very difficult. Many documents about the plans and the actions taken will have been publicly available for months or even years, and copies could be anywhere. Although civil servants, under pressure, may consider the possibility of destroying or manipulating relevant documents, they will realise that doing so is a dangerous gamble. Destroying documents is a crime, and because of the acute risk of being discovered, hardly anyone dares try. That is the Swedish experience.

As an example, in the 1980s three Swedish ministers of justice were fired – three in a row – because they had done something unacceptable and proof was available in official documents. None of them attempted, while under pressure, to manipulate the content of the documents.

Thus, freedom of information laws are extremely valuable to journalists – and to citizens in general – when they need clarity about mistakes or wrongdoing by civil servants that are unplanned. Laws on openness do also have a limiting effect on planned wrongdoing, such as corruption, but more indirectly and in the long term. Officials carefully planning to do what is not allowed will of course, as far as possible, avoid putting incriminating facts into official documents. However, creating an atmosphere of openness, a sense among civil servants of always performing on stage, will over time diminish the temptation to do what is forbidden.

Finally, there is the No answer. The Swedish transparency model does not always work in the sense that it sometimes tends to have an undesirable effect: information relevant to citizens may be omitted from official documents. It has been argued that public officials generally will document their work poorly when they sense a risk of unfavourable attention or publicity. Poor documentation may of course indicate unwanted, unethical or even criminal intention, but does not always signal suspect behaviour. Civil servants might simply find it easier to do the job without concerned citizens or journalists – the latter feeding on conflict – monitoring their activities.

Transparency and media coverage of the public sector

When a parliament adopts legislation on citizen access to official documents, the arguments are usually about accountability and the aim of strengthening citizens' trust in state and local authorities.

As mentioned previously, a great number of countries have during the last 15 years engaged in openness reform. Researchers have been quick to evaluate these legislative efforts.[62]

What the studies show is not encouraging in every way. Citizens' trust in government agencies is, after a few years of transparency, not

---

62. Fung A., Graham M. and Weil D. (2007), *Full disclosure. The perils and promise of transparency*, Cambridge University Press, Cambridge; Hood C. and Heald D. (eds) (2006), *Transparency. The key to better governance?* Oxford University Press, Oxford; Roberts, A. (2006), *Blacked out. Government secrecy in the Information Age.* Cambridge University Press, Cambridge; Florini A. (ed.) (2007), *The right to know. Transparency for an open world.* Columbia University Press, New York.

strengthened in many countries. There are no reliable statistics, but in many places the average citizen actually has become more suspicious and negative towards government agencies. This should not come as a surprise, considering the way news reporting is conducted today.

In the richer parts of the world, and increasingly in the not-so-rich parts, people live in societies where the media are a dominant force. What citizens learn about the world beyond their local neighbourhood – about the region, the country, the world – they learn from the media. The Internet has not changed this situation. The basic principles of news reporting are no secret. A government agency doing what it should, in an effective manner, is unlikely to draw the attention of journalists. Who buys a newspaper to read stories about that?

Journalists typically start paying attention to government agencies when, somewhere, something is not going well. Consequently, when things have gone wrong, and journalists have a right to access information about what happened, there will be more negative news about government activities than before. Covering up, hiding mistakes, was often possible when the administration worked behind closed doors. Now this is no longer possible where information can be accessed.

It could be argued however, that researchers are looking for results too early and, more importantly, that they have been looking for the wrong kind of results. Political cultures and administrative traditions will not change from one year to the next. At this stage it might be more rewarding for researchers, when studying the effects of modern transparency reform, to focus on the actual performance of civil servants rather than on what insufficiently informed citizens believe about that performance.

It must be acknowledged, though, that journalism is a part of the problem. In Europe and North America at least, the commercialisation of journalism blurs the line between the entertainment and news reporting industries. When "news" becomes just another commodity in a market of "information products", journalists find it increasingly difficult to claim to be doing their job in the democratic process. That job means, on the ideological level, providing citizens with the kind of information about their society that helps them understand it, and ultimately make crucial decisions. When selling news stories becomes the dominant reason for producing them, the democratic function is easily lost. When selling, your task is to provide the buyer with what he or she wants. In journalism, it will either be stories that flatter the customers, that support their preconceived notions and their prejudices, or stories that shock them or call for outrage whether there is reason for it or not.

And as with all industrial production in a competitive environment, the costs for producing news must be cut to the lowest level possible. As cutting costs inevitably means that journalists must produce more "content" and more news within a shorter time span, the quality is likely to deteriorate and the nature of the news will change. Serious, thorough journalistic work tends to take time, and the number of journalists engaging in this kind of work is decreasing.

But if journalism is part of the problem, it must also be part of the solution. The quality of the information provided to citizens must be high, and the costs for keeping it high must be met by someone. It must be stressed though, that stronger government control over news reporting cannot be the solution. Journalism must be independent in order to function as a pillar of democracy.

The quality of future journalism is worth mentioning as a reminder of the complexity of any successful transparency reform. Openness must be seen as a regime, a system consisting of several legal, administrative and political components supporting each other. Passing a law on access to official documents may actually be the easier task. Implementing an open government regime takes more effort.

The future of transparency

The number of countries that have adopted some kind of access legislation should be cause for optimism. The ideal of transparency seems to have swept the world. However, there are clouds on the horizon.

The fact that citizens' trust in government agencies in many cases actually decreases as a first effect of journalists' access to publicly held information is a problem. That finding will not seem encouraging to parliamentarians in countries considering new or radicalised transparency reform.

Another problematic aspect, with regards to transparency, is globalisation. Globalisation may be both necessary and rewarding in many aspects, but one of its effects is that governments that are forced to "open up" to international co-operation lose control over decision-making processes. In a world where nations and economies are increasingly dependent on each other, national leaders and parliaments have shrinking remits within which they are free to make decisions. Transparency is about ensuring that citizens understand how and why important political decisions are made, but when decision making moves to international levels and is the result of politically sensitive negotiations, transparency does not move with it.

The World Bank, the International Monetary Fund, the World Trade Organization, the North Atlantic Treaty Organization, the United Nations and a number of other international bodies make decisions that have far-reaching effects on nations and their citizens. The decision-making processes within these organisations are rarely "open" in a real sense. And today, of the 100 largest economic bodies in the world, more than half are not nations but multinational corporations. They are not open.

In 1995 Sweden joined the EU, and has since allowed considerable decision-making powers to be transferred to that higher political level. It has created what is usually described as a "democratic deficit", as most Swedes find it extremely difficult to follow political debate and decisions within the EU. The previously mentioned regulation on citizens' right to access EU documents has done little to change this. For a number of reasons, real transparency is hard to realise in a political body of this kind. The differences in political cultures are significant among the nations of the EU. There are language barriers to bridge and there are no European newspapers, television or arenas for political debate. Again, access rights are important, but insufficient.

On the subject of future challenges for transparency enthusiasts, let us not forget that the societal forces opposing open government are both strong and persistent. This is certainly true in Sweden, and I am sure it is true for most countries. As with free speech and other civil rights, access to official documents needs constant protection. Forces advocating a more closed society will always be at work. People and organisations that have won a battle for openness will constantly have to defend what they have just accomplished. Have no illusions: it is a never-ending struggle.

Conclusions

The Swedish experience from two centuries of transparency within authorities at all levels is clearly positive. Open government promotes fair and equal treatment under the law and efficiency in public administration – and it strengthens democracy. However, the concept of transparency is complex. Granting citizens rights to access official documents is crucial, but rarely enough to achieve the goal of transparency.

Citizens must be able to find the documents they need to see. Thus, strict rules for government agencies on how to register their documents and obligations to help citizens find what they are looking for are important. Strong legal protection for journalists' sources – in this context, particularly for public officials assisting the media – is also a vital component of transparency. Vigorous institutions (such as the courts and ombudsmen) supervising the transparency regime are another.

The reach of access rights requires continuous scrutiny and debate. In particular, the right of one citizen to access information about another is a key issue when determining the level of openness. Applying strict data-protection principles when deciding on limits to citizens' right to access official documents may at first glance seem preferable, but it is important to realise that it also severely limits the positive effects of transparency.

Chapter 4:
Media pluralism and human rights

Miklós Haraszti, former OSCE Representative on Freedom of the Media, writer, journalist, human rights advocate and university professor

> Free expression and the free imparting of information are, first and foremost, individual rights. But media pluralism is the institutional guarantee of their fulfilment.

Photo © Shutterstock.

Summary

Media pluralism is the key that unlocks the door of freedom of information and freedom of speech. It advances the ends of freedom of speech by facilitating a robust marketplace of ideas and placing additional checks on the power of states. And it contributes to the development of informed and diverse societies. But because the goal of achieving pluralism places obligations on governments, the notion remains hotly debated both intellectually and politically. What exactly is meant by the term "media pluralism"? How successfully is media pluralism protected in Europe today? And in what ways can media pluralism be advanced in the future in the context of changing technology and changing views about the role of governments? This chapter sets out to answer these questions, and more.

The chapter is split into five sections. Section one offers a theoretical, legal and historical background to the idea of media pluralism. Having sketched a definition of media pluralism, the relationship between freedom of speech and media pluralism is explored. It is observed that media pluralism (or a lack thereof) is a real problem in Europe today, and that it is imperative for governments to work towards achieving media pluralism. That imperative is supported by legal standards that protect media pluralism, which are outlined in this section. An attempt is also made to trace the history of media pluralism, and to explain why it has taken so long for media pluralism's relationship with freedom of speech to be properly understood. Section one helps to place media pluralism in a broader context.

Section two examines media pluralism trends in the Council of Europe member states. It observes encouraging patterns, for instance, in the move towards diversified media ownership and the rise of public service broadcasting in some places. However, it also highlights causes for concern – such as monopolisation of broadcasting, a lack of ownership transparency, and the rise of bureaucratic harassment and administrative discrimination. Exactly what measures are required by human rights standards are reiterated here. It is pointed out that governments have a duty to foster media pluralism, and that this extends to many different dimensions of pluralism. Section two focuses on media pluralism "on the ground", and how standards on paper are being translated into practice.

In section three the central obstacle to pluralism of the media – its monopolisation – is probed more deeply. The case is made for regulation of media ownership, and some of the harms of media monopolies are discussed with reference to the post-Soviet democracies and Italy. This section underscores the need for policy change and action by governments on media pluralism.

Section four turns to further challenges and solutions for the future to guarantee media pluralism. These include rethinking the media as more than just a market, securing the independence of regulators, developing robust media organisations, building public service broadcasting, and engaging with challenges emerging with the rise of the Internet. This section makes clear that media pluralism can be achieved with careful thinking and responsible governance. Conclusions are presented in section five.

Introduction

In today's societies, the basic human right to freedom of expression and information cannot be properly exercised without the presence of a large number of rival media outlets which are free from the domination of political or commercial interests. Free speech, even if constitutionally granted, becomes a mockery if reduced to the information flow available through a few "authorised" or "winning" outlets. Access to a great variety of media is not just necessary for free speech; it is also crucial to make democracy work. Only a sufficiently diverse media environment can keep the public aware of facts, views and debates which hold governments to account.

Defining media pluralism

The media are pluralistic if they are multi-centred and diverse enough to host an informed, uninhibited and inclusive discussion of matters of public interest at all times.

Pluralism of the media means a media structure that is:

- comprised of competing media outlets which are independent from each other or a central owner;
- diversified on separate but overlapping planes of ownership, political views, cultural outlooks and regional interests;
- able to communicate to all corners of society;
- capable of conveying a great variety of information and opinion;
- designed to draw information from a wealth of different sources.

The relationship between free expression, freedom of information and pluralism of the media

Pluralism is an effect of freedom of speech but it is also a value associated with free speech itself. A multi-centred diversity of media outlets is an important prerequisite for free speech.

Freedom of expression and freedom of information – the freedoms "to hold opinions without interference and to seek, receive and impart information and ideas" are basic human rights as set out in 1948 by the Universal Declaration of Human Rights (see Article 19). Since then, international and local human rights standards have acknowledged that freedom of speech must be accompanied by media freedom and media pluralism.

Free speech and information do not occur naturally. They are values that are achieved with the assistance of the free media. If media diversity fades, even constitutionally granted speech freedoms can become meaningless and disappear. The pyramid of free expression, free flow of information and pluralism of the media comprises a crucial prerequisite for achieving and maintaining democracy.

Whereas freedom of expression might be thought of as "the right to speak", and freedom of information can be characterised as "the right to know", pluralism of the media could be considered "the right to choose".

Free expression and the free imparting of information are, first and foremost, individual rights. But media pluralism is the institutional guarantee of their fulfilment. Pluralism is a quality of democratic societies, as well as an individual human right that can be enforced through juridical, constitutional and international mechanisms.

Media pluralism:
theoretical, legal and historical context

Nobody can guarantee that every media outlet can be "free" in the sense that each outlet is independent from any extra-journalistic, political or economic influences. Only dictatorships dare to claim they can "guarantee" an information flow that serves the common good; that promise has always turned into suppression of what people really think, know and would like to say.

But there are very real threats, even in open societies, to the development of a free and pluralistic media. The natural tendency in any political and commercial competition for the more powerful competitors to seek to own, dominate or at least influence social communication can harm media competition. Domination of the media by a small number of bodies – what might be called "media monopolisation" – can also have the effect of suppressing what people can think, know or say.

Because of these trends, it is not enough for governments to exercise self-restraint in the hope that the media will be able to do their job. Governments have an obligation to secure freedom of the media without interfering, that is, with the help of laws and policies that sustainably uphold multi-centred diversity.

Media pluralism is society's next best alternative to what is impossible to achieve perfectly: absolute freedom and independence of individual media outlets. Imagine a country where all media outlets are turned by their owners into propaganda mouthpieces or just careless, unethical money-making machines. In that hypothetical country, it is not the government's enforcement of community standards that will rescue the possibility of ethical, professional journalism. It is the encouragement of competition and diversification.

This hypothetical situation is not far from the reality in many places. In societies recovering from periods of dictatorship, pluralism has assumed a special strategic importance. In such places, the apparent end of "big", governmental censorship has disappointingly only led to "small", private mini-censorships, maintained this time by media-owning entrepreneurs and parties. Audiences who previously hated the monotony of a directed press have found the cacophony of freedom startling. They may have become irritated by the swift spread of commercialism and the slow increase in ethical journalism. In new democracies, it has been hard for audiences to acknowledge that press freedom may make quality journalism possible – but does not guarantee it.

In these places, with faith in democracy at stake, it is imperative for governments to react not by promising "proper" and "honest" journalism enforced by law, but by ensuring that no parts of the spectrum are allowed to dominate the others, and by simultaneously employing positive measures, such as the establishment of well-funded, independent public service broadcasters that serve as positive examples of diverse and fair journalism.

Because of the ongoing dangers of media monopolisation, upholding diversity is not just society's next best alternative to absolute freedom; pluralism is in fact the ultimate guarantee of any freedom of speech. As a structural condition for the whole of the press, it lays down the main rule of the game: diversity. It is then up to the different media enterprises and audiences to build diversity in terms of political, cultural and other outlooks.

Legal standards relating to media pluralism

Freedom of expression, the free flow of information, and freedom and pluralism of the media have internationally been acknowledged as human rights in the post-Second World War intergovernmental instruments: the Universal Declaration of Human Rights (UDHR, 1948) and the International Covenant on Civil and Political Rights (ICCPR, 1966). In both the UDHR and the ICCPR, Article 19 makes this commitment.

In Europe, the specific provision serving as the binding guarantee of those rights is Article 10 of the European Convention on Human Rights (ECHR, 1950). The European Union (EU) has also included free speech rights in its Charter of Fundamental Rights (2000). The specific references to these rights are reproduced in Figure 1.

Figure 1: Media pluralism in international law

Article 19 UDHR 1948
Everyone has the right to freedom of opinion and expression; this right includes freedom to hold opinions without interference and to seek, receive and impart information and ideas *through any media* and regardless of frontiers.

Article 19 (2) ICCPR 1966
Everyone shall have the right to freedom of expression; this right shall include freedom to seek, receive and impart information and ideas of all kinds, regardless of frontiers, *either orally, in writing or in print, in the form of art, or through any other media of his choice.*

Article 10 (1) ECHR 1950-53
Freedom of expression
1. Everyone has the right to freedom of expression. This right shall include freedom to hold opinions and to receive and impart information and ideas without interference by public authority and regardless of frontiers. *This article shall not prevent States from requiring the licensing of broadcasting, television or cinema enterprises.*

Article 11 Charter of Fundamental Rights of the European Union 2000-09
Freedom of expression and information
1. Everyone has the right to freedom of expression. This right shall include freedom to hold opinions and to receive and impart information and ideas without interference by public authority and regardless of frontiers.

2. *The freedom and pluralism of the media shall be respected.*[63]

(Emphases added)

---

63. "Paragraph 2 of this Article spells out the consequences of paragraph 1 regarding freedom of the media." See the European Parliament's explanation of the Charter: www.europarl.europa.eu/charter/pdf/04473_en.pdf.

A short history of media pluralism

Media pluralism has had an interesting journey in achieving its status today as an indispensable human right. Both Article 19 of the UDHR and Article 19 of the ICCPR stress that the right to free expression and the free flow of information is only possible if society has free access to a multitude of media, and if society has a free choice between different media outlets (see relevant emphases in Figure 1).

However, it was only in the television era that the notion of media pluralism was given greater prominence in the standard-setting documents of the United States of America and Europe. During this period media pluralism was cast as a basic social precondition and constituting element of the human right to free expression and freedom of information.

In Europe, Article 10 of the ECHR was originally sparse in its references to media freedom and pluralism. It even found it necessary to stress the member states' right to restrict (license) broadcasting (see relevant emphasis in Figure 1).

Nevertheless, the notion of media freedom and pluralism has been, since the 1950s, developed in the constitutional law of several countries, with France, Germany and the United Kingdom leading the way. Over time, the various mechanisms of the Council of Europe have provided powerful and detailed elaboration of pluralism as a right corollary to, and inseparable from, the right to freedom of expression promulgated by Article 10 of the ECHR.

This standard-setting work has made it clear that the silence on media diversity in Article 10 was not because of any disdain for the idea of media diversity, but was instead because media diversity was simply not seen as a problem in the period preceding the authorisation of privately owned television in Europe.

Three of the Council of Europe institutions improved the situation over the years: the case law of the European Court of Human Rights, several seminal recommendations by the Committee of Ministers, and resolutions by the Parliamentary Assembly. The 27 members of the EU secured a separate entry for media pluralism in the Charter of Fundamental Rights of the European Union (conceived in 2000), putting it on an equal footing with the other two basic free speech human rights, free expression and the free flow of information (Article 11, "The freedom and pluralism of the media shall be respected.") This came into force through the Treaty of Lisbon in 2009.

Why did media diversity become protected as an explicit human right some time after the recognition of free expression and the free flow of information? The answer lies in the fact that, starting from the era of broadcasting (in a departure from the era of the printing press), the monopolisation of the flow of information has become a genuine danger even in democracies.

In the 1950s, when the American invention of television broadcasting – operated there as a business scheme – was imported to Europe, it was initially placed under government control everywhere. That was due to the high investment costs of entry into the market, costs which were especially large in European states that had a much smaller market than the USA. It was also because of the acknowledged power of the audiovisual media to persuade and influence. The spectre of the totalitarian past and the dangers of irresponsible propagandising (arising from uncontrolled broadcasting) were undoubtedly in the minds of some of governments.

For a long time, up until the 1980s, state-sponsored broadcasting was the norm in Europe, and privately owned television the exception. Across the two sides of the Iron Curtain, the only – but crucial – difference in the understanding of state monopoly of broadcasting was that in the West, following the example of the British Broadcasting Corporation (BBC), broadcasting was expected to be an autonomous public service, a provider of "internally pluralistic" (pluralism within a single medium) information for the satisfaction of all sides of the political spectrum; while in the Soviet-dominated parts of Europe, it openly and even proudly served as a propaganda tool of one-party governments. However, in Western Europe in the early 1980s, and after the democratic upheavals of the late 1980s across the rest of the continent, state domination of broadcasting became untenable, and privately owned stations had to be allowed – if not for other reasons, then simply because audiences demanded variety.

By 1993, when the Strasbourg Court delivered its judgment on *Informationsverein Lentia and Others v. Austria*[64] holding that Austria's prohibition on privately owned licences was in breach of Article 10 of the ECHR, it remained virtually the only western European country left with a state monopoly of broadcasting. (This point is taken up in greater detail below.) The argument, once invoked in good faith to allow only one broadcaster per country – that it is imperative to keep television protected from any type of domination – had now been turned against all governmental, ownership, market-share or other types of information monopolies.

The political context: the role of government in media pluralism

The development of media technology played a role in the transition to media pluralism; licensing became inevitable as the number of available frequencies and channels grew. But the need for strict governmental enforcement of pluralism via licensing did not disappear. In stark contrast to the unruly, editorially partisan media outlets mushrooming on today's global networks, satellite television and the Internet, the requirement of internal pluralism for nation-based broadcasting channels remained intact. This was because of the transmitting medium of "pre-digital" broadcasting. Only a small number of analogous frequencies could be allocated, limited by the size of European countries, while broadcasting's political influence stayed constant. There emerged a need for regulators to monitor whether the allocation of licences was efficiently serving the goals of ownership, political, cultural and regional diversity.

The further development of technology, especially after the Europe-wide digital switchover is complete in 2012, may lead to another

---

64. *Informationsverein Lentia v. Austria*, Commission Report of 9 September 1992, Appl. Nos. 13914/88, 15041/89.

surprising change in pluralism governance. It will put an end to a world of scarce frequencies. It will no longer be impossible to achieve the near-perfect "external pluralism" (pluralism across multiple outlets) which has hitherto justified regulatory control over not only the public service but also licensed television. In the digital and Internet era, with the number of accessible channels and audiovisual platforms multiplying by the year, urgency for detailed regulation – the bulk of which is aimed at avoiding political domination – will fade. At the same time, the danger of regulatory intrusion may loom larger.

Pluralism governance remains as important as it used to be, but its focus may shift towards securing external pluralism of the media, and a fuller access to all media platforms for all kinds of content providers (social and cultural) and for minorities. This would support the fulfilment of another set of human rights related to pluralism: the free expression of cultural, religious, minority or local content providers, which may be able to gain a better foothold than in the "analogue frequency era".

Surprisingly, however, the need for public service broadcasting could make a comeback, even as the Internet portal and aggregator sites become suppliers of a new style of internal pluralism, which so far has been expected from television channels. Excessive fragmentation of information can pose a threat to the quality of democracy's public sphere, as can the monopolisation of that information. Hence a taxpayer-funded – and preferably advertisement-free – universally accessible safe haven for fair and inclusive audiovisual information, coupled with an online equivalent, may become imperative again, especially during election periods.

The role of governments in television may, therefore, return to its European origins, providing for a national infrastructure of seasoned, independent editorial work, based on the best of journalistic ethics. A platform for guaranteed pluralistic information is as important today, when public service broadcasting may be but an island in the ocean of content providers, as it was in the 1950s, when the public service broadcasters were the Europeans' only audiovisual outlets.

Media pluralism trends in the Council of Europe region

Soon after the Soviet Union broke up, almost all of territorial Europe had united under the banner of democracy. In the 1990s, freedoms such as the right to free elections, free civil society and free speech were acknowledged by all Council of Europe nations. Symbolising the end of the "poles apart" systemic divisions, these nations voluntarily accepted the Council of Europe's intergovernmental scrutiny of their human rights record.

The state of play on media pluralism

By and large, Europe today is a continent of freedom of expression and media pluralism, especially compared to its past. There is no nation in the Council of Europe territory where the laws deny outright the right of independent outlets to operate. Nor is there any nation in the Council of Europe region without the presence of at least a few independent print press outlets. However, Belarus (though not itself a member state of the Council of Europe), Russia and the South Caucasus are some areas in the Council of Europe region where, despite the allowances for advertisement-fuelled private licences, there exist no television broadcasters with an editorial line independent of the government position.

But Europe's apparent unity masks serious discrepancies in how the shared standards are actually applied on the ground. In fact, in many new democracies in Europe, media diversity is in poor shape, due to a lack of regulatory policy focused on boosting pluralism. These deficiencies are not just signs of developmental delay. Unfortunately, they are reflections of the governments' desire to continue monopolising ownership or just to control the press, and thereby exclude critical voices from accessing the media.

In western Europe "consolidation" into ever larger ownership blocks is the greatest threat, but this threat is for the most part handled quite well by regulators. Thanks to the EU, issues of media ownership and market share have become supranational on one level while remaining political issues at home. This system provides fairly good protection against monopolies, although there is still room for outliers like Italy – a case study that is explored later in this chapter.

The situation in central and southern Europe reminds us that mere variety is not sufficient if the media is to play a robust role in helping to maintain democracy. Here, anti-monopoly legislation works, and the full spectrum of opinions is accessible. Privatisation is complete and state ownership of the media is over; public service television exists, though it is far from autonomous. However, the press, and increasingly television as well, are partisan or even party-owned; a growing number of media outlets are offshoot investments and status symbols of personal power. The Italian model has followers, in that media magnates aim at political influence, the actual creation of political parties, or both. This seems to be appealing especially in smaller nations where an overcrowded, pre-consolidation market is the current norm (while many states, especially in the Balkans, represent so tiny a market that they would have trouble sustaining a media industry even after its de-politicisation and healthy collapse into fewer units). Journalism, therefore, when not utterly commercial, is utterly partisan, judgmental and contrarian – a constant competition of blistering adjectives, slanted invective and spin wars. Put simply, central Europe has a type of media pluralism that is reminiscent of the famously confrontational mentality of the pre-1933 German democracy.

After the transition to liberal democracy, central European media embraced freedom and provided a common ground for debate and discussion. Twenty years later this openness and understanding has been eclipsed by a spirit of confrontation and polarisation. In such circumstances, foreign ownership of the local media, provided it is properly diversified – and it mostly is – can be a blessing. Central Europe's media have been rescued from landing in the hands of local, parochial, non-media investors only by the presence of foreign owners. Foreign-owned media also provides a safe haven amongst the media from fragmentation into antagonistic political camps, a fragmentation that was once so typical of eastern Europe. The foreign-owned outlets have never engaged in racist, extremist or even tendentiously biased journalism. This is probably so, not out of an innate idealism but out of the necessity to make money: foreign owners, unlike local oligarchs, have to earn media money too, and not just spend it.

This is where EU membership counts, with its facilitation of both foreign ownership and its commitment to breaking up monopolies. The EU has empowered commissioners and special mechanisms to react to complaints of monopolisation of media and related markets, such as content production, transmission technology or communications platforms. The boundaries to be maintained are of course under constant public examination and are often redefined. At the time of writing, for example, there is much criticism that the British and international media empire of Rupert Murdoch has been under less scrutiny from the European Commission than the efforts by Spain and France to de-commercialise their national public service broadcasters by collecting a modest fee from commercial media ventures. Paradoxically, these pioneering measures have been seen by the Commission as thwarting competition, even though they could also be interpreted as improving competition and enhancing pluralism. In fact, in exchange for the small fee, commercial media rid themselves of a major competitor in advertising. Guaranteeing at least one channel of advertisement-free quality television is an important element of cultural diversity.

In the former Soviet nations, however, except for the Baltic states which are today members of the EU, it seems that there is a trend that the more significant role a media type plays in providing citizens with political information, the less pluralistic it is allowed to be.

This tendency is particularly obvious in television. In most post-Soviet nations, the attempt to break up broadcasting monopolies has failed. Except for Ukraine and Georgia, nowhere in the former Soviet Union is a degree of pluralism in television tolerated. Even in those two countries, the situation is quite similar to the polarised central European media scene.

Both in terms of ownership and content, television in the post-Soviet states is firmly in the hands of the administration or friends and family members of government leaders. This is so regardless of whether television is outright state-owned or under partly private ownership; it is regardless, too, of whether or not (so-called) public service television exists.

Furthermore, the privately owned press and television are in the hands of local non-media investors. The media oligarchs are, as a rule, those who also invest in the media. The very idea of foreign media ownership is treated by the governments of most of these states as anti-patriotic.

Russia, which due to its large territory could have allowed for a variety of television channels even via classic analogue transmission, now has effectively only a few nationwide channels. All of these channels are state-owned or state dominated. What is more, the state energy monopoly has devoured the small amount of television variety that did exist in the first decade after the political changes. Gazprom-Media has, in effect, re-nationalised television.

Public service television is practically non-existent outside the EU. Moldova and the South Caucasus countries are the only post-Soviet nations that have decided to establish such taxpayer-funded yet autonomous broadcasting channels. But with governments reluctant to allow them to do their job, of providing guaranteed internal pluralism of news and opinions for all sides of the political spectrum, there has been manipulation that has ensured that members of boards, CEOs and editors toe the line. These moves have in effect turned public service broadcasters into state-run institutions from the outset.

Those regulatory agencies that supervise and license privately owned broadcast media are also not independent in this region. All boards are dominated by the government. Regulators are not mandated to license specifically for the establishment of pluralism in the airwaves. Licensing is an exercise in thinly veiled arbitrariness and nepotism. Ownership transparency, the most important administrative tool for breaking up monopolies, is either not mentioned in law or not enforced by regulators. Nominal owners do not even pretend that their position is anything more than nominal.

In many post-Soviet countries, a key component of the pre-democracy media structure still exists: the state-owned print press. As a rule, the privatisation of the print press is not only far from complete, a huge amount of taxpayer money is poured into the state and municipality-owned print press.

Many post-Soviet states have a "grants for content" system set up by presidential decrees, which is designed to be a tool of (print) media support. But, in defiance of the requirement of a platform- and content-neutral media support system, the payouts hardly benefit pluralistic production; in most cases, the grants are used to reward content that the government approves of. Moreover, advertisement revenue from state-owned companies is channelled to the state-owned papers, or to the private domain, in exchange for favourable editorial policies.

Still, thanks to the changes that took place two decades ago, a degree of media pluralism does exist in the post-Soviet countries as well. At this point, however, pluralism is confined to the financially fragile independent print press. Overshadowed by the broadcast media and in many places by the state-owned print press, such press outlets reach very limited audiences. This is partly due to the general crisis of the newspaper industry, but also because of government-induced action.

The independent print media (and generally, the laws and institutions facilitating start-up media enterprise and market entry) face administrative discrimination. Distribution and subscription operations, including news and magazine kiosks, are run as monopolies in many states. "Information ministries" and equivalent agencies, equipped with arbitrary decision-making powers, are firmly in control of registration procedures and all other processes necessary for the birth and survival of independent media outlets.

Belarus is the chief inventor of the system of bureaucratic harassment that, over the course of the last decade, has decimated politically independent media outlets in many countries in the post-Soviet region. The calculating methods employed in this system include official registration of outlets, which transforms registration into official permission to publish; mandatory re-registration when the government calls for it; and the government's right to warn and close down papers for "misuse of freedom of the press" – that is, for unwanted content.

The Internet remains the only source of truly pluralistic information; but even Internet freedom may only be enjoying a short grace period in the eyes of many governments. Already, Internet Service Provider

(ISP) pluralism is in danger: one central state-controlled ISP per country is the norm. With the help of a state monopoly of ISPs, in the absence of the legally secured competitive private ownership of ISPs, the global network can be fragmented into nationally controlled spaces. An ISP monopoly opens the way towards state control of content, typically resulting in an arbitrary reduction in the Internet's innate pluralism. State filtering and blocking is increasingly the fashion, as is the creation of arbitrary legal backing for it. Still, the Internet is the hottest battlefield. And higher penetration, digitalisation and the ensuing abundance of communication channels may eventually end up being the transformation that renders futile the current efforts to achieve media monopolisation.

In all these battles for true pluralism, international standards, and especially those specified by the different mechanisms of the Council of Europe, play a crucial role.

The need for human rights law, standards and policy in Europe today

Both the Council of Europe and the EU are clear in underscoring the role that pluralism plays in ensuring basic human rights to free expression and the free flow of information.

The Committee of Ministers of the Council of Europe has stated that "media pluralism and diversity of media content are essential for the functioning of a democratic society and are the corollaries of the fundamental right to freedom of expression and information."[65] The Charter of Fundamental Rights of the European Union indicates that "the freedom and pluralism of the media shall be respected."[66] Both proceed to point out that core freedoms (of speech, of information,

---

65. Committee of Ministers Recommendation CM/Rec(2007)2 on media pluralism and diversity of media content, 31 January 2007. See also the similar Committee of Ministers Recommendation No. R (99) 1 on measures to promote media pluralism, adopted on 19 January 1999.
66. Article 11, paragraph 2, freedom of expression and information, (2000/C 364/1). See: www.europarl.europa.eu/charter/pdf/text_en.pdf.

and, indeed, even of the media) can be best protected by boosting a pluralism that is able to serve society's actual diversity.

The Council of Europe in particular, tasked by its member states to set the standards of what human rights and democracy require from European governments, has developed over the last 30 years a quite vast array of case law, guidelines and recommendations that help governments to deal with the different aspects of media pluralism in a fast-changing world.

As early as 1977, the European Court and Commission of Human Rights[67] stated that Article 10 of the ECHR imposes positive obligations on member states to take action and not merely to refrain from interference.[68] The Committee of Ministers specified in 1982 the nature of that obligation, by calling on nations to "adopt policies designed to foster as much as possible a variety of media and a plurality of information sources, thereby allowing a plurality of ideas and opinions."[69] The European Court of Human Rights has also referred to "the principle of pluralism, of which the State is the ultimate guarantor."[70]

Proactive care for pluralism requires governments to implement regulations relevant to the different media spheres, as well as targeted policies aimed at upholding media choice and access. An example is how the aforementioned, pathbreaking 1993 Lentia judgment of the Strasbourg Court also embarked on the exploration of the specific policies to be implemented for the sake of pluralism. It added that the observation about the duty of governments "is especially valid in relation to audiovisual media, whose programmes are often broadcast very widely."

---

67. This institution was abolished in 1998. Its role was to act as an intermediary between claimants and the Strasbourg Court: if it thought a claim was well-founded, it could launch a claim on a claimant's behalf.

68. *de Geillustreerde Pers v. the Netherlands*, Committee of Ministers DH (77) 1, 17 February 1977.

69. Declaration on the freedom of expression and information (Adopted by the Committee of Ministers on 29 April 1982 at its 70th Session).

70. *Informationsverein Lentia v. Austria*, Appl. Nos. 13914/88, 15041/89, 15717/89, 15779/89 and 17207/90, judgment of 24 November 1993, paragraph 38.

An even more specific obligation, to ensure pluralism within the broadcast media during election periods, has been addressed in a Council of Europe recommendation: "During election campaigns, regulatory frameworks should encourage and facilitate the pluralistic expression of opinions via the broadcast media."[71] It is especially crucial to maintain the diversity of information regarding facts and opinions about government, that is, in the "market" of political discourse.

An equally important "positive" goal is to make the media accessible not only for the news and views of the ready-made political blocs of the day, or for the social, ethnic, religious or other constant majorities, but also for all sorts of minorities.

The different kinds of media pluralism today

The shorthand term "media pluralism" encompasses everything from media types, interests such as ownership and control over the media, political and cultural viewpoints, and regional concerns, all of which have to be communicated or accessed through the media. The various documents of the Council of Europe and the EU refer to several dimensions of media pluralism, such as: internal and external pluralism; cultural and political pluralism; open and representative pluralism; and structural and content pluralism.[72]

Access can be both active and passive. External diversity could occur across media sectors or just a specific segment, such as print or television. Internal pluralism concerns diversity within a single media outlet.

In countries where media pluralism is pursued in earnest, one can see evidence of two basic approaches. There is the "marketplace of ideas" model. Then there is "public sphere" media model, in which democracy requires the unifying, rational public discourse of the

---

71. Committee of Ministers Recommendation No. R (99) 15, Appendix, II(1).
72. See for instance the Committee of Ministers Recommendation CM/Rec(2007)2 on media pluralism and diversity of media content, adopted on 31 January 2007; and Committee of Ministers Recommendation No. R (99) 1 on measures to promote media pluralism, adopted on 19 January 1999.

citizens.[73] Both are meant to serve the public good, the former with the competition and freedom of choice, the latter in its aim to provide the whole of society with political views and cultural values.

Regulatory approaches, regardless of theories, must combine the two, just as the standards of the Council of Europe do, since in a democracy both external and internal pluralisms have to be functional. Diversity sometimes is best achieved when people can freely enter the "marketplace of ideas" without any governmental constraints; at other times and in other places, the survival of various political views and cultural values necessitates state intervention.

The standards also stress, of course, that more regulation is not better regulation. Governmental self-restraint remains the default rule, as with everything that concerns free speech. Excessive regulation may be harmful for media pluralism, as it may suppress legitimate choices and stifle innovation.

Challenge of monopolies: regulation of media ownership

Freedom of expression is only possible under a media market that is not marred by a monopoly. Ownership control is the starting point of pluralism governance; it ensures that free speech is not diminished by the overbearing control of too few media entrepreneurs or too few actual media outlets. Attempts to break down media monopolies have to be directed towards all significant information markets, and focused on ownership, media types, political viewpoints, cultural outlooks and regions.

It is especially crucial to establish limits for the participants in markets where, for technical reasons, only a few players can be licensed. The best-known example is the medium with the greatest impact, television, the supremacy of which is continuing even as its transmission technology is changing. Until recently, it had to be transmitted via analogous surface frequencies that were available in a limited range, meaning only a few stations could operate in a region, as well as nationwide.

---

73. Habermas J. (1962), *Struktuwandel der Öffentlichkeit*, Hermann Luchterhand Verlag, Darmstadt.

European standards adopt methods of assessment of undue concentration of ownership that include audience or market share, rather than just numerical limitations on how many channels an individual or company can own. The Committee of Ministers has urged "the adoption of rules aimed at limiting the influence which a single person, company or group may have in one or more media sectors as well as ensuring a sufficient number of diverse media outlets."[74] Most EU member states have adopted media ownership regulations according to this recommendation.[75] The limitations apply to ownership within print, broadcasting or other sectors; cross-ownership in two or more sectors; and media integration with other industries such as phone networks or advertising.[76]

The Council of Europe encourages the use of "thresholds based on objective and realistic criteria, such as the audience share, circulation, turnover/revenue, the share capital or voting rights."[77] It is interesting to note what amounts to a dominant position for such thresholds. The European Commission guidelines draw that line at 40%, despite the fact that the everyday notion of such a position is more than 50% of market share.[78]

---

74. Committee of Ministers Recommendation CM/Rec(2007)2 on media pluralism and diversity of media content, adopted on 31 January 2007, I (2.1).

75. K.U. Leuven/ICRI/Jönköping International Business School/MMTC/Central European University/CMCS/Ernst & Young Consultancy Belgium (2009), *Independent study on indicators for media pluralism in the member states – Towards a risk-based approach*, Leuven, p. 31, see: http://ec.europa.eu/information_society/media_taskforce/pluralism/study/index_en.htm.

76. Ibid., Annex III: Country inventories of legal and policy measures promoting/supporting media pluralism, p. 784, see: http://ec.europa.eu/information_society/media_taskforce/doc/pluralism/study/part_3.pdf.

77. Committee of Ministers Recommendation CM/Rec(2007)2, adopted on 31 January 2007, I (2.3).

78. "Guidelines on market analysis and the assessment of significant market power under the Community regulatory framework for electronic communications networks and services" (2002/C 165/03), paragraph 75, see: http://eur-lex.europa.eu/LexUriServ/LexUriServ.do?uri=OJ:C:2002:165:0006:0031:EN:PDF.

Developments in media technology and economy suggest that ownership control remains even more relevant in the digital era. It is in broadcasting that monopolies have their gravest effect on freedom of expression, as television remains the main source of information in all nations. A look at the negative impact of broadcast monopolies on democracies suggests that they are potentially as dangerous as the erstwhile perils of outright state censorship.

Negative impact of media monopolies in new democracies

In the new democracies of the post-Soviet region, one finds government-owned networks which are not public service networks. Private licensees of commercial televisions often turn out to be government-friendly oligarchic groups in various disguises. Quite a few of these owners also play a major role in politics.

Across the region, lingering state ownership of the media produces the bulk of available information, making the media a matter of command line in terms of its content, and a matter of the subsidy in terms of its funding – both controlled from the top. Privatisation, licensing and digital switchover procedures are not required or even allowed to aim at achieving diversity. The activity of the boards and offices mandated to undertake these crucial transformations are often overtly nepotistic.

Specifically, tacit re-nationalisation of broadcasting has taken place in Russia, where the state energy body Gazprom was allowed to found a powerful "private" media arm, Gazprom-Media. It has purchased many formerly privatised print titles, radio channels and even nationwide television channels. The South Caucasus republics of Armenia, Azerbaijan and Georgia have suffered from a lack of ownership transparency. Only in 2011 did Georgia finally pass clear and more enforceable rules.[79]

---

79. The legislation requires broadcasting companies to make public information about their owners and sources of finance and prohibits the offshore ownership of television stations: see, for instance, www.dc4mf.org/en/content/georgia-passes-law-make-media-ownership-more-transparent.

The case of Italy

The history of the so-called "Italian anomaly" is illustrative of how broadcast monopolisation (through over-consolidation and super-mergers) can pose an acute danger even in older democracies.[80]

Freedom of expression and press freedoms are in a healthy state in Italy. However, the television broadcasting market is regularly referred to as the "Italian anomaly".

In the last two decades, no third force has been able to constrain the so-called duopoly: domination of the nationwide television channel market by the private owner, Mediaset, and the public owner Radiotelevisione Italiana, RAI. The duopoly was accompanied by a practical monopoly by Mediaset in the commercial television sector and the advertisement market. Before digitalisation, the duopoly's audience share was around 90% (both owned three channels). Combined revenues and the advertisement market also provided evidence of the duopoly.

Italy also has an ongoing record of control over public service television by political parties and governments. As its Prime Minister Silvio Berlusconi co-owns Mediaset, the usual fears of governmental control of RAI are aggravated by worries of widespread governmental control of the nation's most important source of information, television.

The so-called Gasparri and Frattini Laws of 2004 were supposed to provide guarantees for future pluralism of the media, and outlaw "two-hat" situations, respectively. However, neither universal digitalisation nor equal competition rules alone can guarantee cultural diversity and political pluralism in the media, especially if the already existing media concentration is practically maintained or even enhanced by

---

80. See Miklós Haraszti's 2005 report, see: www.osce.org/fom/46497. See also the chapter on Italy in Open Society Foundations (2005), "Television across Europe: Regulation, policy and independence", as updated by 2008's "Television across Europe: Follow-up reports", Italy chapter. Both are available at www.mediapolicy.org. Further, see written comments by the Open Society Justice Initiative (March 2010) in the case of *Centro Europa 7 v. Italy* in the European Court of Human Rights, Appl. No. 38433/09, see : www.mcreporter.info/documenti/osji_eu7.pdf.

the law. The Gasparri Law's rules of transition from analogue to digital, despite their innovative force, allow the duopoly to use its acquired economic might to expand into new digital markets.

European standards prohibit undue political or partisan ownership or control of private broadcasters in order to avoid government or political interference. Germany and the UK impose restrictions on direct owner-ship or control of broadcast media by political actors; EU countries also require broadcasters to maintain independence from political parties and politicians. Italy, despite its Frattini Law, does neither.[81]

Further challenges: media more than just a market

Notwithstanding the importance of anti-competition legislation, the media should not be viewed as just another market; its pluralism must be about content and access, decisive values for democracy's public discourse. General competition policy, even a fair market share arrangement, is not conceived for, and is rarely able to, fulfil the func-tion of protecting the diversity which human rights standards demand.

The objective is to move beyond "freedom from" ownership mono-polies to a "freedom to" society's right to access a diverse information flow, multi-centred enough to sustain unfettered public debate on all important issues. At issue is freedom of political expression and an informed citizenry.[82]

This is why human rights standards highlight the responsibility of governments to focus on information monopolies in the media, not just ownership monopolies. In too many countries, even those in which a seemingly diversely owned media exists, the content falls into two categories: it is either pro-government or purely entertainment. Different mechanisms and institutions in addition to anti-competitive policies are needed so that a variety of media is able to serve society.

---

81. K.U. Leuven–ICRI, op. cit. (note 75), Annex III, p. 782.
82. "Free political debate is at the very core of the concept of a democratic society." *Lingens v. Austria*, Appl. No. 9815/82, judgment of 8 July 1986, paragraph 42; *Castells v. Spain*, Appl. No. 11798/85, judgment of 23 April 1992, para. 43.

Securing the independence of regulators

The regulators which authorise and supervise broadcasting must in all their rules and practices aim at the desired end-goal: pluralism.

The arcane rules of licensing, from the composition of boards to the criteria for the evaluation of licensees, and the lack of public oversight of decisions, offer myriad possibilities for governments which are less than eager to cede control of television.

If boards are politically partisan, licensing criteria arbitrary or vague, and operation or judicial oversight weak, content pluralism might disappear, at least from television, despite diversified ownership.[83] The aim is to keep government or its associates from doing the job in a self-interested way. This aim can usually be achieved by setting up autonomous and inclusive licensing boards.

As the Committee of Ministers has noted, "the rules governing regulatory authorities for the broadcasting sector, especially their membership, are a key element of their independence. Therefore, they should be defined so as to protect them against any interference, in particular by political forces or economic interests."[84]

One of the many examples of government shortcomings is the lack of clear ownership transparency rules, or the lack of enforcement of such rules. It is impossible to break up monopolies or regain trust in media freedom if society is not allowed to know who the ultimate owners of the broadcasting firms are.[85]

---

83. For examples of these dangers in Hungary's media laws passed in 2010, see: "Notes on Hungary's media law package", at www.eurozine.com/articles/2011-03-01-haraszti-en.html.

84. Declaration of the Committee of Ministers on the independence and functions of regulatory authorities for the broadcasting sector, adopted on 26 March 2008, see: https://wcd.coe.int/wcd/ViewDoc.jsp?Ref=Decl%2826.03.2008%29.

85. For an excellent general discussion of the related issues, see: Mendel T. (2002) "Access to the airwaves: Principles on freedom of expression and broadcast regulation", *International Standards Series*, ARTICLE 19, London, at www.article19.org/pdfs/standards/accessairwaves.pdf.

Developing robust media organisations

Although the principle of pluralism disallows owners or outlets from becoming too powerful, it nevertheless requires strong media enterprises that can successfully compete and maintain their independence in the face of political or commercial pressures.

Crises of secure funding often hit the print press, which is the most eminent source of quality ethical journalism and is crucial for democracy's rational and informed debates. One wave of the crises came with the advent of television, and another is sweeping through the industry right now with the dawn of the digital era.

In addition to the worldwide crisis of the print press industry, the downward trends in media pluralism are often accompanied by upward trends in media business. In many countries, the independent print press is kept financially fragile by various means.

There are countries where the privately owned media have to endure administrative discrimination in every aspect of their operations. Some of these ill-conceived policies artificially delay the privatisation of state-owned press. Start-up activities may be made impossible due to discriminatory taxation, registration and licensing rules. It is not only in Italy that one finds oligarchic investment. Also hindering the strength of the media are non-media investments, made by banking, real estate or energy firms.

When journalists are criminalised under journalistic or non-journalist pretexts, it is usually the independent media that are targeted. The same is true of violence against journalists. The impunity that follows these acts also weakens the independent press.

There are natural reasons, too, for this state of fragility. For example, the small-size markets of south-eastern European countries such as "the former Yugoslav Republic of Macedonia", Montenegro or Kosovo* are finding it hard to supply their media with advertisement revenues.

---

* All reference to Kosovo, whether to the territory, institutions or population, in this text shall be understood in full compliance with United Nations Security Council Resolution 1244 and without prejudice to the status of Kosovo.

In order to prevent such fragility, regulation may draw on taxpayer-funded support. However, these subsidies must be content-neutral and pluralistic. The Parliamentary Assembly of the Council of Europe has encouraged governments to provide economic aid for the embattled print industry, while warning of the need to "avoid arbitrary exclusion from governmental aid programmes of periodicals published by opposition forces".[86] It has also recommended that any form of selective aid be administered only by an independent body.[87]

Public service broadcasting in the service of pluralism

The European standards for pluralism traditionally prescribe the founding of publicly funded broadcasting institutions tasked to provide internal pluralism of news and views. Both the formidable role of television in shaping public opinion, and the difficulties of achieving external pluralism in relatively small European markets, require every nation of Europe to set up at least one strong, easily accessible audiovisual infrastructure for objective news and reliably inclusive public journalism.

These broadcasters function as a "public service", catering to all citizens. They have received constitutional backing in most European nations, and have become a symbol of shared European cultural identity.

Public service broadcasters (PSB) operate autonomously but are regulated by detailed statutes. This is another complex part of television governance: the "science" and "politics" of establishing inclusive governing boards and funding schemes. These should keep broadcasters editorially independent of government, internally pluralistic and able to withstand the competition from their commercial counterparts.

Different standard-setting institutions of the Council of Europe have provided detailed and constantly upgraded guidelines on PSB, seeing

---

86. PACE Recommendation 747 (1975) on press concentrations, see : http://assembly. coe.int/main.asp?Link=/documents/adoptedtext/ta75/erec747.htm.
87. PACE Recommendation 834 (1978) on threats to the freedom of the press and television, see: http://assembly.coe.int/mainf.asp?Link=/documents/adoptedtext/ ta78/erec834.htm.

it as an eminent tool of building trust in democracy; complementing external pluralism of the privately owned media; and supporting the positive, social goals of pluralism.

External and internal pluralism:
a European-type "dual broadcasting system"

When the innovations of radio and TV were first imported from the United States, they were made a government monopoly even in democracies. Since the 1980s, the "dual" (or mixed) regime has been designed to guarantee both internal and external pluralism. The dual system institutionalises the coexistence of a publicly founded BBC-type PSB that is accessible to all, with US-type commercial, privately owned broadcasting.

American scepticism about the dilemma of government-regulated internal pluralism or public journalism regulated in law (which raises the question, "can the government really defend us from governmental influence?") is not unwarranted in the light of experience, and not only in the new democracies. Provided it works, PSB is an eminent tool to uphold democracy in smaller, fragile democracies.

The dual system is an ideal combination of external and internal pluralism. While the commercial, private media may work on the notion of "one man, one vote", highlighting the values of their own viewers in their quest for revenues and newsworthiness, PSB can be a guaranteed infrastructure for detached, impartial newscasts both in times of and between elections, more reliable than governments, parties or the market.

PSB's inclusive remit[88] also provides a unique opportunity to strengthen all types of human rights, the rule of law, democracy and the protection of minorities. It is a unique platform for the achievement of societal goals such as civility, social cohesion, non-aggression and multicultural values.

The guidelines of the Council of Europe on PSB are among the most elaborate and detailed in existence. Their strong points are on PSB's

---

88. Committee of Ministers Recommendation CM/Rec(2007)3 Committee of Ministers on the remit of public service media in the information society, see: https://wcd.coe.int/wcd/ViewDoc.jsp?id=1089759.

legal framework;[89] independence in editorial matters, made possible by the independence and inclusivity of its governance (steering boards);[90] and its multiple-source funding.[91]

The importance of the institution is by no means fading in the digital era. In fact, PSB is transforming into "PSM": Public Service Media. Member states should ensure that existing public service media organisations occupy a visible place in the new media landscape. Social cohesion across all communities, social groups and generations can be supported through the careful use of PSB.[92]

Moving from state to public broadcasting in new democracies

The Council of Europe has also addressed the problems caused by the difficulties of transition from state to public broadcasting in new democracies. This transition has not been a success story.

Russia and Belarus have not even nominally founded PSBs yet. They have state channels that, in terms of political information offer choice, but only between sly propaganda and silly celebrities. PSB has been in the process of protracted legislative development in Ukraine. Moldova's PSB has struggled with political pressures.

The South Caucasus republics have created these institutions, but in practice, at least in Armenia and Azerbaijan, they are just a version

---

89. According to the Committee of Ministers Recommendation No. R (96) 10, the legal framework governing public service broadcasting organisations should clearly stipulate their independence.
90. Among others, see: Committee of Ministers Recommendation No. R (96) 10 on the guarantee of the independence of public service broadcasting; Declaration of the Committee of Ministers on the guarantee of the independence of public service broadcasting in the member states, adopted on 27 September 2006, see: https://wcd. coe.int/wcd/ViewDoc.jsp?Ref=Decl-27.09.2006.
91. PACE Recommendation 1878 (2009) on funding of public service broadcasting, see: http://assembly.coe.int/Mainf.asp?link=/Documents/AdoptedText/ta09/ EREC1878.htm.
92. Committee of Ministers Recommendation CM/Rec(2007)3 on the remit of public service media in the information society, see: https://wcd.coe.int/wcd/ViewDoc. jsp?id=1089759.

of the old state TV concept, not really lending support to pluralism's cause. Opposition news is often news against the opposition. Georgia's PSB had a similar crisis period of political pressure between 2007 and 2010, but now seems to be recovering.

But the status of PSB is not much more robust in the post-1989 democracies that are members of the EU. A case in point is Hungary's PSB, which has been thoroughly re-nationalised following 2010 laws, and put under the command of a Media Council that consists solely of ruling party delegates.

The public and the political community of the new democracies, despite the difficulties caused by lack of consensus among rival parties, are convinced of the benefits of a real PSB, and cherish the creators of real public service programming. They accept the ideally human rights-centred political and cultural values of PSB. This makes it all the more necessary that the Council of Europe guidelines (and other international standards) are applied in these countries.

Pluralism in the age of the Internet

What is needed to achieve pluralism has changed as different forms of media have been spawned. While the print press was still the main market for information, standards for breaking up monopolies were not as demanding. Regulation expanded with the advent of broadcasting and television in particular. With the development of new media, regulation has become vast, but is still easily circumvented.

The Europe-wide switch – "The Switchover" – from analogue terrestrial distribution of broadcasting signals to digitally transcribed or produced transmission signals is supposed to be completed by 31 December 2011, the date suggested by the EU Commission. This move will not only multiply the number of available channels but clearly enhance the chances of external pluralism as well.

In the era of digital convergence markets, the Internet will become the backbone of democracies' information systems. It is the carrier of an ever growing multitude of new media forms while it devours old printed and audiovisual media formats. Information flow can become (and is becoming) truly global, instantaneous and interactive. It is the audiences themselves – each and every citizen – that can become the producers of information. Editorial staff are being replaced by networks.

Democracy has been given new tools, although an unexpected danger for the public sphere has also emerged: excessive fragmentation of the information flow. Under such circumstances, the old formula of pluralism is not sufficient any more. Networking is a force of life in itself, with social media and journalistic media not quite clear yet about each other's role. Time may further detach or fuse them. Still, the rights to free expression, the free flow of information and the notion of pluralism may need to be supplemented with a new tenet, "the right to connect".

A number of governments react to the development of the Internet in much the same way as they reacted to broadcasting in the mid-20th century: with state control. But the human right to free expression today demands that the governments give the "right to connect" the same proactive protection that media diversity enjoyed in the pre-digital era. They must guarantee, as part of the right to free expression, the access of citizens to the global network.

One of the great changes under way is from scarcity to abundance. New media and communication technologies have the ability to spread content across multiple platforms, and have the capacity to support the emergence of many new content creators. The Internet-based media have become a safe haven for truly pluralistic news, but these changes also pose new potential threats to pluralism.

It might appear that nothing can stand in the way of pluralism. In reality, precluding monopolisation of ISPs is as important in the new era as television's diversification has been in the past. As noted, ISP plurality is hindered in many new democracies where deregulation is missing. Freedom from state filtering and blocking is dwindling, while mandatory blocking of content by the ISPs is a frequent legislative proposal.

The need for media providers on all platforms to have equal opportunities may become a seminal new issue. Mobile phones are today's cables

– should their operators have the right to define what's downloadable? Economic interest notwithstanding, pluralism's answer is clear: there must be platform neutrality. And both the Council of Europe[93] and the EU[94] are deeply involved in the debate over new standards, which would give effect to these principles.

Conclusions

What emerges from all of this is a sense that media pluralism is an issue that is both theoretically complex (in the way in which it is nested among other concepts about freedom of speech and the free flow of information) and practically relevant for Council of Europe member states (given the imminent dangers of media monopolisation).

However, the fact that this issue is so nuanced and so significant in the real world should not deter anyone from attempting a clear-headed examination of the current problems and the future solutions surrounding media pluralism. Indeed, it makes that lucid analysis even more necessary.

---

93. Declaration of the Committee of Ministers on network neutrality, adopted on 29 September 2010, see: https://wcd.coe.int/wcd/ViewDoc.jsp?id=1678287.
94. European Commission (2011), "The open internet and net neutrality in Europe", Communication from the Commission, COM(2011) 222 final, see: http://ec.europa.eu/information_society/policy/ecomm/doc/library/communications_reports/net neutrality/comm-19042011.pdf.

Chapter 5:
Public service media and human rights

Boyko Boev, Senior Legal Officer, ARTICLE 19
JUDr Barbora Bukovska, Senior Director for Law and Policy,
ARTICLE 19

> Public service media will be able to contribute
> significantly to the full realisation of human rights
> in society.

*Public service media suggest a shift to a broader media landscape, encompassing
traditional public service broadcasting and new communication services. They use digital
media and platforms, including the Internet, instead of just broadcast television or radio.
Photo © Council of Europe.*

Summary

The future of public service media (PSM) is unclear. At present, two general scenarios are under discussion in Europe. The first is optimistic: it refers to PSM's importance for the cultural heritage of the country. The second is pessimistic and claims that the public service broadcasting model is outdated, idealistic and expensive with no future in the digital age. The aim of this chapter is to contribute to the current debates by suggesting the "rights-based approach" to PSM.

Section one highlights developments and challenges to PSM today and their consequences on the free flow of information and human rights. Media regulators, broadcasters, politicians and the public seek responses to the following four challenges faced by PSM: transformation from public service broadcasting to PSM; explosive competition at production and transmission; securing the right level of independence from the state, private competitors and interest groups; and securing public support and public funding for PSM. These challenges, arising from technological developments, competition and calls for PSM accountability, can improve the free flow of information.

At the same time, there is a real danger that in the process of digitalisation and the introduction of new technologies some groups will be cut off from the information flow in PSM. Competition with private broadcasters and the demands for funding can result in less media pluralism and can degrade the quality of audiovisual works. Insufficient funding can be a barrier for language and cultural diversity.

In section two, we present the specific aspects of the rights-based approach to development. We argue that the analysis of PSM stakeholders' rights and duties should be used in PSM governance because it is a very useful political, economic and social test for taking decisions and for evaluating their outcomes. This approach can develop accountability, participation, non-discrimination and empowerment in the field of PSM. It can improve PSM image and performance by advocating interactive and inclusive systems of governance and programme policies. Most importantly, rights can empower those who are involved in PSM and create a strong initiative for public participation and focus on the most disadvantaged.

Section three outlines current initiatives to improve PSM at European and national levels that concentrate on addressing the role of PSM in the digital era, PSM governance and ensuring the independence of PSM.

Section four contains recommendations for a rights-based approach to PSM. These include, among others, the development of indicators for a rights-based approach to PSM and taking human rights into account in PSM legislation and policies. In this section, we conclude that the rights-based approach to PSM policy offers transformative solutions of vital importance for the future of PSM.

Introduction

PSM are media that produce and transmit public-interest content, are funded by the state or the public and have boards appointed by public bodies. The concept of PSM suggests a shift to a broader media landscape. In comparison with public service broadcasting, it has a much wider scope in terms of services, distribution, consumption and interaction as it uses digital media and platforms, including the Internet, instead of just broadcast television or radio. PSM encompasses traditional public service broadcasting and new communication services.

While PSM are well established in some countries, in others they are at different stages in their implementation and development. PSM systems operate in different cultural contexts and have different traditions. They are characterised by a variety of legal approaches vis-à-vis their role, remit and independence and use different models of governance. As there is no common media market in Europe, PSM have varying levels of resources. Arguments have been made for policymakers to restructure and rethink what PSM are and create new forms of systems that are inclusive, innovative and community oriented.[95]

---

95. For example, there have been initiatives to expand traditional PSM functions to include more outreach and co-operation with other institutions such as museums and libraries, and developing joint community outreach initiatives. These efforts aim to make media more relevant to individual concerns and communities.

Still, PSM systems have some common characteristics. The first is that PSM are a part of the "tripartite" system, in which public service and commercial media exist together with community media.[96] The second feature is the general availability of PSM as a direct consequence of their public nature; PSM should be generally available to and accessible by everyone in the country, regardless of location and income. The third feature is the specific public remit of PSM; in general, the aim of PSM is not only to provide all of society with information, culture, education and entertainment, but also promote democratic values, citizenship and social cohesion. The fourth feature is the need for their independence from both state and commercial interests. Although in several countries PSM institutions have been highly politicised and governments have attempted to interfere with their editorial independence, it is generally understood that PSM institutions should not be subject to state control. Commercial independence requires that PSM institutions should not have to compete for funds in the same way as the private media. A fifth feature is impartiality. PSM should present information objectively and dispassionately, should treat all opinions even-handedly and should represent the concerns and interests of as many social groups as possible. Finally, PSM systems should be publicly accountable for their programmes and operation.[97]

At present, two general scenarios for the future of PSM are under discussion in Europe. The first is optimistic: it refers to PSM's importance for the cultural heritage of the country and maintains that "with the right values ... it can have an equally wonderful future too."[98] The second scenario is pessimistic: claiming that the tradi-

---

96. See the Committee of Ministers Declaration on the role of community media in promoting social cohesion and intercultural dialogue, adopted on 11 February 2009 at the 1048th meeting of the Ministers' Deputies. In the Declaration the Committee of Ministers recognises "community media as a distinct media sector, alongside public service and private commercial media".
97. See PACE Recommendation 1878 (2009), paragraph 5.
98. See the speech of Mark Thompson, BBC Director General, "Public media in a digital age" given at the New America Foundation, Washington DC, on 5 October 2001, available at: www.bbc.co.uk/pressoffice/speeches/stories/thompson_naf.shtml.

tional public service broadcasting model is outdated, idealistic and expensive with no future in the digital age.[99]

In the light of these conflicting scenarios, stakeholders are discussing different approaches to PSM systems and governance. In this chapter, we aim to make a contribution to these debates by suggesting the "rights-based approach" to PSM. We believe that the rights-based approach, applied extensively to many other areas of human development, can make a distinctive and vital contribution to PSM as well. Rights are very useful political, economic and social tests for taking decisions and for evaluating their outcomes. Additionally, rights can empower those who are involved in PSM and create a strong initiative for public participation and focus on the most disadvantaged.

The concept of the rights-based approach applies international human rights standards to various processes of human development. In this approach to PSM policies and functions, the primary goal would be to fulfil human rights: that is, primarily the right to freedom of expression but also other rights such as the right to education, the right to public participation, the right to freedom of association and others. There has been little or no work carried out so far on how a rights-based approach can be applied to PSM. Hence, we argue that applying this concept to PSM, by satisfying its five principles (rights, accountability, empowerment, participation, non-discrimination and inclusion of vulnerable groups), will allow it to contribute significantly to the full realisation of human rights in society.

In discussing human rights obligations, this chapter refers to the human rights standards contained in, and principles derived from, international human rights instruments, particularly the International Covenant on Civil and Political Rights (ICCPR),[100] the International

---

99. This view is noted in the Political Declaration, adopted in Reykjavik at the 1st Council of Europe Conference of Ministers responsible for Media and New Communication Services, held on 28 and 29 May 2009, in Reykjavik, Iceland, MCM(2009)011, paragraph 4, available at: www.coe.int/t/dghl/standardsetting/media/MCM%282009%29011_en_final_web.pdf.
100. UN General Assembly Resolution 2200A (XXI), 16 December 1966, entered into force on 23 March 1976.

Covenant on Economic, Social and Cultural Rights (ICESCR),[101] the Convention on Human Rights and Fundamental Freedoms (ECHR)[102] and the European Social Charter (revised),[103] and the UNESCO Convention on the Protection and Promotion of the Diversity of Cultural Expressions.[104]

We also refer to a number of instruments developed and adopted by the Council of Europe in relation to freedom of expression and public service broadcasting.[105]

---

101. UN General Assembly Resolution 2200A (XXI), 16 December 1966, entered into on force 3 January 1976.

102. Adopted on 4 November 1950, CETS No. 5, entered into force on 3 September 1953.

103. Adopted on 3 May 1996, CETS No. 163, entered into force on 1 July 1999.

104. Adopted on 20 October 2005, entered into force on 18 March 2007.

105 Particular references are made to Parliamentary Assembly of the Council of Europe (PACE) Resolution 428 (1970), containing a declaration on mass communication and human rights and setting out principles relating to the status and independence of the media; Recommendation 1407 (1999), defining the role of the media in the development of democracy; Resolution 1636 (2008), listing 27 basic principles for national media legislation and practice; Recommendation No. R (97) 21, containing means of action for promotion by the media of a culture of tolerance; Recommendation No. R (99) 1, proposing measures for promotion of media pluralism; Recommendation No. R (2003) 9, setting out principles for transition to digital broadcasting; Recommendation CM/Rec(2007)2, including measures for media pluralism and diversity of media content; the Declaration of the Committee of Ministers of 31 January 2007, recognising the role of PSM in counterbalancing the risk of misuse of power by the media in a situation of strong media concentration; and the Political Declaration and Action Plan and Resolution "Towards a new notion of media" by the Ministers responsible for Media and New Communication Services. Specific Council of Europe documents concerning the functions and operation of PSM include Recommendation 1641 (2004), reviewing the situation of PSM across Europe; Recommendation 1878 (2009), outlining the key issues related to PSM and their funding; Committee of Ministers Recommendation No. R (96) 10, including guidelines on the guarantee of the independence of public service broadcasting; Recommendation CM/Rec(2007)3, setting out principles concerning the remit of PSM; and Declaration of the Committee of Ministers of 27 September 2006 containing an overview of the independence of PSM in Europe.

Challenges to public service media today and their impact on the free flow of information and human rights

PSM exist everywhere in Europe, though their level of development varies between countries. National political and cultural factors and the state of the economy, as well as the size of PSM, influence their institutional organisation, roles and functions.[106] All models in Europe, however, exist today in an environment marked by several common factors. These include:

- a simultaneous offer of a multitude of free private channels;

- reduced advertising revenues due to the current economic recession and the spread of advertising revenues over a wider range of media;

- new technological developments for the creation and distribution of content (on-demand media services, the digital switchover and the Internet);

- changed audience behaviour and user demands for thematic channels and interactive or on-demand services and the utilisation of the Internet as another platform for providing PSM services.[107]

Overall, PSM faces four major challenges today and the solutions require restructuring of governance systems, processes and behaviour.[108]

---

106. See: Lowe G.F. and Nissen C.S. (eds) (2011), *Small among giants: Television broadcasting in smaller countries*, Nordicom, Göteborg, for an excellent analysis on how size matters for how public service broadcasting works and why in Europe.
107. See: Recommendation 1878 (2009).
108. These challenges have been identified by the Council of Europe's Ad hoc Advisory Group on Public Service Media Governance (MC-S-PG) at which ARTICLE 19 has observer status.

Transformation from public service broadcasting to public service media

In the new digital age, public service broadcasting is transforming into PSM, operating in a broader and more interactive media landscape. Digital technologies provide for the possibility of extending the spectrum of public service broadcasting programmes and new services.[109] In line with the objectives of the EU Digital Agenda,[110] PSM should diversify their formats and expand to new platforms such as the Internet, SMS services, web pages and smartphone applications to respond to user demands. For example, young PSM audiences access services on mobile and Internet-based platforms and are keen users of on-demand services. Apart from servicing society and individual citizens in innovative ways, PSM should use new technologies to engage audiences and enable their participation in content creation and distribution. PSM are expected to play a pioneering role in both encouraging and using technological developments in order to offer their content to the public.[111] The transformation from public service broadcasting to PSM demands appropriate legal frameworks and sufficient financial revenues. It is necessary for states to amend their broadcasting laws to deal with investment and social and technical issues arising from the digital switchover.[112]

Explosive competition at production and transmission

Today public service broadcasters are not the sole broadcasting actors and must compete with other players in the creation and distribution of media content. As noted by the European Parliament:

---

109. By May 2011 the digital switchover had been completely implemented in Andorra, Germany, Denmark, Belgium, Croatia, Slovenia, Finland, Luxembourg, the Netherlands, Sweden, Malta, Latvia, Estonia, Spain and Switzerland.
110. European Commission (2011), "A digital agenda for Europe", Communication from the Commission, COM(2010) 245 final/2.
111. See: Resolution on public service broadcasting in the digital era: the future of the dual system, adopted on 25 November 2010 in a plenary session of the EU Parliament, NI/2010/2028. The resolution was based on a motion and explanatory report prepared by Ivo Belet.
112. See: Nyman-Metcalf K. and Richter A. (2010), *Guide to the digital switchover*, OSCE, Vienna.

Media policy in 2010 cannot be restricted to maintaining the balance between commercial and public service broadcasting. In the current media context, new big players such as telecom and Internet service providers as well as search engines play an increasingly important role. Citizen journalism and user-generated content also challenge the traditional media players. The dual broadcasting system has evolved into a multi-player media environment.[113]

In the new media environment, PSM should ensure a diverse range of freely accessible programming, which contributes to media pluralism, cultural and linguistic diversity, editorial competition and freedom of expression.[114] At the same time state aid for PSM should not result in unfair competition with commercial broadcasters. To prevent unfair competition the EU requires its member states to adopt some form of *ex ante* test and clearly define the public service benefit before launching new services.[115]

Securing the right level of independence from the state, private competitors and interest groups

Technological developments and the liberalisation and opening up of the airwaves to commercial and community broadcasting have not significantly lessened government control over PSM super-visory bodies.[116] For example, a recent study by the Institute of

---

113. Supra, note 111.

114. Supra, note 111.

115. According to paragraph 88 of the Communication from the Commission on the application of State aid rules to public service broadcasting (OJ C 257, 27.10.2009, p. 1), the *ex ante* assessment shall include two steps:

1. Assessment of whether the new services meet the democratic, social and cultural needs of society ("public value"). The assessment of the public character of a service is within the competence of Member States.

2. Assessment of the impact of the service on the market. In assessing the impact of the service on the market, Member States have to take into account a number of criteria (the existence of similar or substitutable offers, editorial competition, market structure, market position of the public service broadcaster, level of competition and potential impact on private initiatives).

116. See for examples of governmental interference with PSM: PACE Recommendation 1641 (2004) on public service broadcasting; Declaration of the Committee of

European Media Law revealed political influence on the Albanian public broadcaster RTSH especially during election periods.[117] In Bosnia and Herzegovina political parties attempt, in parliament, to appoint "their people" to the steering boards of PSM.[118] In Kosovo, the deputy head of the government influenced the nominations for elections to the board of RTK, the Kosovo public service broadcaster, by taking part in the last round of nominations discussed by the responsible parliamentary committee.[119] In Romania, PSM are controlled by the parties with a majority in parliament; the latter can dismiss the PSM board by not approving an annual activity report, and can both nominate and elect the board, whose chairman is also an executive director of PSM.[120]

According to the Council of Europe Recommendation Rec(96)10[121] the legal framework of PSM should contain a number of safeguards against interference, including a clear statement about institutional autonomy, determining the scope of the latter. It should also include particular safeguards against politically motivated appointments or removals of members of governing bodies. It should similarly guard against conflicts of interest on PSM boards. PSM laws should ensure that the funding of PSM is not used to prejudice their independence, and that the pay and benefit packages for the members of the governing bodies are adequate and not determined by the government.

Ministers on the guarantee of the independence of public service broadcasting in member states, adopted on 27 September 2006; Declaration of the Committee of Ministers on the independence and functions of regulatory authorities for the broadcasting sector, adopted on 26 March 2008; Martin B., Scheuer A. and Bron C. (eds) (2011), "The media in South-East Europe", *A Comparative Media Law and Policy Study*, Friedrich Ebert Foundation, Berlin, available at: www.fes.bg/files/custom/library/2011/The%20Media%20in%20South-East%20Europe.pdf.

117. Martin, et al., p. 36.
118. Ibid., p. 44.
119. Ibid., p. 80.
120. Ibid., p. 120.
121. Recommendation No. R (96) 10 of the Committee of Ministers on the guarantee of the independence of public service broadcasting and the Appendix to it.

Securing public support and public funding for public service media

With the huge growth in the number of commercial channels the need for PSM has been questioned in some countries. In addition, some European PSM systems are in urgent need of proper financial backing.

PSM financing is dependent on public support. Some PSM are financially unstable as a result of the low collection rate of broadcasting fees. For example in Serbia, the collection rate is 44%, and thus far from sufficient to cover PSM expenses.[122] Another problem is dwindling public resources in many countries, which prevent PSM from maintaining the level and quality of programming required. However, if PSM are allowed to supplement their income with external funding they may become subservient to their backers. In Bulgaria, for instance, the lack of a clear and transparent funding scheme makes PSM funding dependent on the goodwill of the government and parliament.[123]

Without stable and sufficient funding, PSM will not be able migrate to the digital media environment and fulfil their remit. Moreover, scarce and unstable funding increases the risk of interference with editorial independence.

The responses to the weaknesses of the current models of funding include the improvement of management to efficiently use all available resources, increasing skills and retaining talent, and ensuring an appropriate level of public accountability by developing more transparency and responsiveness.

We believe that the above challenges, arising from technological developments, competition and calls for PSM accountability, can improve the free flow of information through:

– digitalisation and new technologies that help PSM fulfil their duty to promote free expression, quality journalism, pluralism and democratic values in innovative ways. Various groups, including minorities whose needs are served inefficiently in purely commercial markets, can have different access to PSM information and programmes;

---

122. Martin et al., op. cit., p. 126.
123. Ibid., p. 57.

- competition and co-operation with other media that leads to the improvement of content and to mixing private media ownership with public service values. Private media companies with public service values have become important players in several media markets, including the United Kingdom (Channel 4), Sweden (TV4) and Norway (TV2). The European quotas in favour of independent producers have a positive impact on new players in PSM;[124]

- the launching of new initiatives for transparency and the introduction of new forms of dialogue with the public, which stimulate accountability of both PSM as an institution and the state as a main PSM stakeholder. Democratisation of PSM will ensure more effective and closer engagement with audiences.

Nonetheless, there is a real danger that, in the process of digitalisation and the introduction of new technologies, access to PSM for some groups will be cut off from the flow of information or that not everyone will be able to interact on new platforms or participate in PSM governance. Competition with private broadcasters and the demands for funding can result in less media pluralism and can degrade the quality of audiovisual works. Insufficient funding can be a barrier to language and cultural diversity.[125]

---

124. The Audiovisual Media Services Directive and the Council of Europe Convention on Transfrontier Television elaborate on quotas in favour of independent producers. See Directive 2010/13/EU of the European Parliament and of the Council of 10 March 2010 on the coordination of certain provisions laid down by law, regulation or administrative action in Member States concerning the provision of audiovisual media services (Audiovisual Media Services Directive) and the European Convention on Transfrontier Television, adopted on 5 June 1989, text amended according to the provisions of the Protocol (ETS No. 171), which entered into force on 1 March 2002.
125. The UNESCO Convention on the Protection and Promotion of the Diversity of Cultural Expressions, adopted on 20 October 2005 by the 33rd General Conference and entered into force on 18 March 2007, recognises the powers of states to adopt policies and measures aiming at protection and promotion of cultural expressions, including enhancing diversity of the media through public service broadcasting. Such measures can include quotas concerning broadcast productions.

Rights-based approach to public service media

In this section, we demonstrate how a rights-based approach can be applied to PSM and argue that it should guide policies and reforms related to PSM.

A rights-based approach is a conceptual framework for a process of development that is based on international human rights standards and directed at promoting and protecting human rights, analysing inequalities, and redressing discriminatory practices and the unjust distribution of power.[126] Borrowing from this concept, the rights-based approach to PSM should be based on:

- linkage to human rights standards: human rights standards contained in, and principles derived from, international human rights instruments, should guide the policy development and implementation of PSM. As such, the rights-based approach to PSM shall identify the rights holders and the duty bearers, and ensure that duty bearers have an obligation to realise all human rights;

- accountability: the state should be accountable for its policy in support of PSM while PSM institutions should be fully accountable for their actions. As duty bearers, state and PSM institutions should be obliged to behave responsibly, seek to represent the greater public interest and be open to public scrutiny;

- participation: the rights-based approach to PSM demands a high degree of participation of all interested parties;

- non-discrimination: principles of non-discrimination, equality and inclusiveness should underlie the practice of PSM. The rights-based approach to PSM should also ensure that particular focus is given to vulnerable groups, to be determined locally, such as minorities, indigenous peoples or persons with disabilities;

- empowerment: the rights-based approach to PSM should empower rights holders to claim and exercise their rights. This

---

126. Human rights-based approaches have been applied to development, education and reproductive health. See: the UN Practitioner's Portal on Human Rights Based Programming: http://hrbaportal.org.

means that there should be mechanisms to compel state and PSM institutions to perform their duties.

Below we examine how these principles can be applied to PSM and used to strengthen PSM policies and reforms.

Linkage to human rights standards

Under the rights-based approach, the main objective of governmental policies relating to PSM would be to respect, fulfil and protect human rights. The right to freedom of expression is the most relevant to PSM, but other rights are also involved.[127]

Right to freedom of expression

Article 10 of the European Convention on Human Rights and Fundamental Freedoms states that:

> 1. Everyone has the right to freedom of expression. This right shall include freedom to hold opinions and to receive and impart information and ideas without interference by public authority and regardless of frontiers. This Article shall not prevent States from requiring the licensing of broadcasting, television or cinema enterprises.

> 2. The exercise of these freedoms, since it carries with it duties and responsibilities, may be subject to such formalities, conditions, restrictions or penalties as are prescribed by law and are necessary in a democratic society, in the interests of national security, territorial integrity or public safety, for the prevention of disorder or crime, for the protection of health or morals, for the protection of the reputation or rights of others, for preventing the disclosure of information received in confidence, or for maintaining the authority and impartiality of the judiciary.

In the *Handyside* case, the European Court of Human Rights underscored the importance of the right to freedom of expression stating that it is one of the "essential foundations of [democratic] society,

---

127. The right to freedom of expression is guaranteed by Article 19 of the International Covenant of Civil and Political Rights, Article 9 of the African Charter on Human and Peoples' Rights, and Article 13 of the American Convention on Human Rights.

one of the basic conditions for its progress and for the development of every man."[128] Furthermore, the Court explained that Article 10 is applicable not only to inoffensive "information" or "ideas" but also to those that "offend, shock or disturb the State or any sector of the population."[129]

Furthermore, the Parliamentary Assembly and the Committee of Ministers of the Council of Europe have promulgated numerous resolutions, declarations and recommendations which elaborate on Article 10's protection for PSM.[130] The Court's judgments and the instruments adopted by the Parliamentary Assembly and the Committee of Ministers over a period of almost 60 years illustrate how the Council of Europe has helped to create viable PSM.

There are a number of points of immediate practical relevance to PSM in Article 10.

The right to freedom of expression belongs to both individuals and the media

Although ECHR does not explicitly mention the freedom of media, the Court grants the press special status in the enjoyment of the freedoms contained in Article 10. In the case of *The Sunday Times* (No. 1)[131] the Court confirmed that the principles relating to freedom of expression defined in the *Handyside* case are applicable to and of particular importance for the press. Furthermore, in the *Jersild* case[132] the Court recognised that the press plays the "vital role of a 'public watchdog'" and emphasised the need for the application of these principles in the area of audiovisual media.[133]

---

128. *Handyside v. the United Kingdom*, Appl. No. 5493/72, judgment of 7 December 1976, paragraph 49.
129. Ibid.
130. See notes 102-5, 110-11, 115-16.
131. *The Sunday Times v. the United Kingdom*, Appl. No. 6538/74, judgment of 26 April 1979, paragraph 65.
132. *Jersild v. Denmark*, Appl. No. 15890/89, judgment of 23 September 1994.
133. Ibid., paragraph 31.

The right to freedom of expression includes the right to impart and receive information and ideas

The right to impart information and ideas which is normally exercised by journalists and the media is complementary to the right of individuals to receive information and ideas.[134] In the *Jersild* case[135] the Court clarified that the protection afforded by Article 10 includes not only the substance of the ideas and information expressed but also the form in which they are conveyed. In this case, the Court found that the Danish courts violated Article 10 when they convicted a journalist employed at the Danish Broadcasting Corporation for his film, which included an interview with a group of young people in the course of which they made racist remarks. The Judges in Strasbourg held that it was not for them or the national courts to substitute their own views for those of the press as to what technique of reporting should be adopted by journalists.[136]

The right to impart and receive information "through any media" enshrines the freedom of broadcasting and the right of access to broadcasting, both private and public. Freedom of expression is expressed not only through private media but also through PSM.

Does the right to freedom of expression entail an individual right to express views and opinions via PSM?

The opinion of the Court on this question was stated in the *Haider* case:[137]

> Article 10 (of the ECHR) cannot be taken to include a general and unfettered right for any private citizen or organisation to have access to

---

134. For the first time the Strasbourg Court recognised the complementary character of the right to impart and the right to receive information and ideas in the *Jersild* case. This position has been reiterated in subsequent cases. See for example, *Radio France and Others v. France*, Appl. No. 53984/00, judgment of 30 March 2004, paragraph 33.
135. *Jersild v. Denmark*, op. cit.
136. Ibid., paragraph 35.
137. *Haider v. Austria*, Appl. No. 25060/94, decision of 18 October 1995 (European Commission of Human Rights).

broadcasting time on radio or television in order to forward his opinion, save under exceptional circumstances, for instance if one political party is excluded from broadcasting facilities at election time while other parties are given broadcasting time.[138]

The right to freedom of expression applies across borders

This point is highly relevant in an age when the technical capacity to broadcast across borders is widely available. In the *Autronic* case,[139] the Court recognised that the right to receive information covers also international television broadcasts.

The right to freedom of expression must be accompanied by the right to protection of journalists' sources

While this right is not explicitly provided by the ECHR and other international human rights treaties, it has been proclaimed in constitutions (for example the constitutions of Portugal and "the former Yugoslav Republic of Macedonia"), general and special laws, and has been recognised by the Court and national courts.[140] Recommendation No. R (2000) 7[141] sets out exceptions to the right to protection of sources where:

–   the identity of the source is necessary for the investigation or prosecution of a serious crime, or the defence of a person accused of a criminal offence;

–   the information or similar information leading to the same result cannot be obtained elsewhere;

138. Ibid., paragraph 3 of the Law Section. The Commission referred to Application No. 9297/81, Dec. 1.3.82, D.R. 28, p. 204 and No. 23550/94, Dec. 24.2.95, unpublished.
139. *Autronic AG v. Switzerland*, Appl. No. 12726/87, judgment of 22 May 1990.
140. In 2007 in its decision in the *Cicero* case (1 BvR 538/06; 1 BvR 2045/06) Germany's Constitutional Court declared the security services searches of a journalist's apartment and the offices of *Cicero* magazine in September 2005 in Potsdam unconstitutional because they aimed "exclusively" or "predominantly" at identifying the source of the media's information, and not at actually pursuing a criminal case.
141. Recommendation No. R (2000) 7 on the right of journalists to disclose their sources of information, adopted by the Committee of Ministers on 8 March 2000, at the 701st meeting of the Ministers' Deputies.

- the public interest in disclosure outweighs the harm to freedom of expression; and
- disclosure has been ordered by a court or another independent or impartial decision-making body, after a full hearing.[142]

States should limit their restrictions to freedom of expression

The ECHR provides that the right to freedom of expression may be restricted only if such a restriction is prescribed by law, pursues a legitimate aim and is necessary in a democratic society to achieve this aim.[143] The Court has examined the legitimacy of various measures in the field of public service broadcasting.

Monopoly of public broadcasting

In the *Informationsverein Lentia* case,[144] the Court found that the state broadcasting monopoly in Austria is a far-reaching restriction on the freedom of expression which was not justified by a pressing need. Therefore, the refusal to provide licences for operation of private television and radio stations was found to be in breach of the right to freedom of expression.

Prohibition of political advertisement

In the *VgT Verein gegen Tierfabriken* case,[145] the Court found that the prohibition on broadcasting a political advertisement via the Swiss Radio and Television Company was not justified with relevant and sufficient arguments and did not answer a particularly pressing social need.[146]

---

142. Ibid., Principle 3.
143. See Article 10 of the ECHR, paragraph 2.
144. *Informationsverein Lentia v. Austria*, Appl. Nos. 13914/88, 15041/89, 15717/89, 15779/89 and 17207/90, judgment of 24 November 1993.
145. *Vgt Verein gegen Tierfabriken v. Switzerland*, Appl. No. 24699/94, judgment of 28 June 2001, paragraph 69.
146. In contrast to the *VgT Verein gegen Tierfabriken* case, in the *Murphy* case the Court held that a ban on broadcasting a radio advertisement for a religious meeting was justifiable under Article 10 of the ECHR. The judges agreed that in the latter case the member states enjoyed a wider margin of appreciation to determine how to balance religious expression with protection of rights of others due to the lack of uniform European conceptions on this topic.

Defamation

In the *Radio France* case,[147] the Court found that the conviction of radio journalists of defamation did not violate Article 10. The judges considered that there was a "pressing social need" to take action against journalists who incorrectly reported that a former deputy prefect had admitted that he supervised the deportation of Jews during the Second World War.

Locking and packing up television after cancellation of subscription of public service television

In the *Faccio* case[148] the Court found that the right to freedom of expression of an applicant was not violated by the police locking and packing up his television after he asked for a cancellation of his subscription to public service television. The Court observed that the action was permitted by a legislative decree which aimed at dissuading individuals from failing to pay the licence fee, which was regarded as a tax for the financing of the public broadcasting service. The Court did not find problematic the obligation for owners of television sets to pay the tax in question regardless of whether or not they wished to watch programmes on public channels.

Disciplinary measure against a journalist employed by PSM

In the *Wojtas-Kaleta* case,[149] the Court found a violation of the right to freedom of expression. A journalist employed by the Polish public television company (TVP) was reprimanded by her employer after criticising the programming of TVP in an interview published in a national newspaper. Accepting that the issues raised by the journalist were of general interest and taking note of the professional obligations and responsibilities of the journalist, the Court determined that in this case the right to freedom of expression outweighed the duties of employees towards their employers.

---

147. *Radio France and Others v. France*, Appl. No. 53984/00, judgment of 30 March 2004, paragraph 37.
148. *Faccio v. Italy*, Appl. No. 33/04, decision of 31 March 2009.
149. *Wojtas-Kaleta v. Poland*, Appl. No. 20436/02, judgment of 16 July 2009.

State obligations with respect to broadcasting pluralism

The state obligation to create an environment in which diverse media exist has been proclaimed by the UNESCO Convention on the Protection and Promotion of the Diversity of Cultural Expression.[150] The convention establishes that states enjoy the sovereign right to adopt measures to protect intercultural dialogue and the diversity of cultural expressions, as well as a duty to adopt measures aimed at enhancing the diversity of media, including through public broadcasting.

Likewise the Committee of Ministers of the Council of Europe stated in Recommendation CM/Rec(2007)2[151] that "Member states should encourage the development of other media capable of making a contribution to pluralism and diversity and providing a space for dialogue. These media could, for example, take the form of community, local, minority or social media."

In the *Wojtas-Kaleta* case,[152] the Court underlined the state's role of guaranteeing pluralism, declaring that "where a State decided to create a public service broadcasting system, the domestic law and practice must guarantee that the system provides a pluralistic audiovisual service."[153]

Other human rights relevant to PSM

States are obliged to respect and protect other rights from the ECHR that are relevant to PSM and their staff. These include the right to life,[154] the prohibition of torture, inhuman and degrading treatment and punishments,[155] the right to liberty and security,[156] the

---

150. UNESCO Convention on the Protection and Promotion of the Diversity of Cultural Expression.
151. Recommendation CM/Rec(2007)2 of the Committee of Ministers on media pluralism and diversity of media content, adopted by the Committee of Ministers on 31 January 2007, at the 985th meeting of the Ministers' Deputies, paragraph 4.
152. *Wojtas-Kaleta v. Poland*, op. cit.
153. Ibid., paragraph 47.
154. European Convention for Human Rights, Article 2.
155. Ibid., Article 3.
156. Ibid., Article 5.

right to privacy[157] and the prohibition on discrimination.[158] Under the European Social Charter, PSM staff are entitled to a number of employment and social rights including freedom to work,[159] fair working conditions,[160] right to association and collective bargaining rights,[161] right to social security, social welfare and social services,[162] and the right to non-discrimination.[163]

The Council of Europe monitors the situation of journalists' rights. Recalling the state's obligation, in accordance with Article 2 and 10 of the ECHR, to prevent and investigate any murders of journalists as well as acts of severe physical violence and death threats against them, Resolution 1535 (2007)[164] of the Parliamentary Assembly highlighted that "where attacks against journalists can be carried out with immunity, democracy and the rule of law suffers."[165]

The 2010 report *Respect for media freedom*,[166] by the Parliamentary Assembly of the Council of Europe (PACE) Committee on Culture, Science and Education, listed cases of death threats, harassment and physical attacks by police officers and individuals against PSM journalists. For example, in Kosovo, a television presenter was threatened in June 2009 following her investigative reports on the public television channel RTK about limits on press freedom in Kosovo and alleged atrocities committed by the Kosovo Liberation Army

---

157. Ibid., Article 8.

158. Ibid., Article 14.

159. European Social Charter, Article 1.

160. Ibid., Article 2.

161. Ibid., Articles 5 and 6.

162. Ibid., Article 12.

163. Ibid., Article 20.

164. Resolution 1535 (2007), adopted by the Parliamentary Assembly on 25 January 2007.

165. In Recommendation 1897 (2010) the Parliamentary Assembly of the Council of Europe recalled that at least 20 journalists have been killed in Europe since 2007 and proclaimed that states must do more to ensure respect the safety of journalists.

166. "Respect for media freedom", Report by Committee on Culture, Science and Education, Doc. 12102, published on 6 January 2010, Rapporteur: Mr Andrew McIntosh, United Kingdom, Socialist Group.

in the conflict of the late 1990s. In 2008 and 2009 bombs were exploded at the EiTB public broadcasting headquarters in Bilbao and another against a television transmission facility in Hernani. The aforementioned PACE report on *Respect for media freedom* included cases in which journalists in Moldova were arrested during post-election demonstrations in April 2009.

The Strasbourg Court has examined complaints on searches of journalists' homes and seizure of their equipment for identification of their sources. In the *Voskuil* case[167] and the *Tillack* case[168] the Court found that searches and seizures at journalists' homes and offices and seizure of their equipment interfered with their right to freedom of expression.

Non-human rights standards related to PSM

Although no international treaty deals explicitly with PSM, the Council of Europe has developed standards defining state-specific obligations with respect to PSM. In addition Council of Europe instruments list the obligations upon PSM organisations.

The first is a general obligation to maintain PSM and the responsibility "to guarantee the fundamental role of the PSM".[169] The Council of Europe instruments elaborate on this obligation by defining several responsibilities. States should:

–   set the remit of PSM. Specific provisions should be included in legislation;[170]

---

167. *Voskuil v. the Netherlands*, Appl. No. 64752/01, judgment of 22 November 2007.
168. *Tillack v. Belgium*, Appl. No. 20477/05, judgment of 27 November 2007.
169. Although most Council of Europe standard-setting instruments concerning PSM describe the PSM characteristics and principles without developing a list of specific state obligations in relation to them, Recommendation No. R (99) 1 and Recommendation CM/Rec(2007)2 are exceptions insofar as they specifically elaborate on member states' obligations towards PSM. See also Recommendation CM/Rec(2007)3 on the remit of public service media in the information society.
170. Recommendation CM/Rec(2007)3 on the remit of public service media in the information society.

- enable PSM to use new communication technologies and services by providing them with the necessary technical resources.[171] In order to ensure universal access to PSM, states should enable public service broadcasters to transmit on the different digital platforms (cable, satellite, terrestrial);[172]

- encourage PSM to play an active role in promoting social cohesion and integration among various societal groups including ethnic and religious minorities, the young, the elderly, the unemployed and persons with disabilities while respecting their different identities and needs.[173] States should ensure that all have universal access to PSM;[174]

- ensure that PSM institutions, organisations and all parties concerned are accountable for their performance. Expectations should be clearly defined, and PSM and other stakeholders should provide effective reporting of performance. States should ensure that PSM regularly make information on their activities available to the public and develop procedures for allowing viewers and listeners to provide feedback;[175]

- support the introduction of public consultation mechanisms which may include the creation of programming policy advisory structures, suitably diverse in their composition to reflect the general public;[176]

- guarantee the independence of PSM from any kind of political or social control, in deciding their internal organisation. States

---

171. See recommended measure V. related to public service broadcasting of Recommendation No. R (99) 1 and Recommendation CM/Rec(2007)2 on media pluralism and diversity of media content.

172. Recommendation Rec(2003)9 on measures to promote the democratic and social contribution of digital broadcasting, adopted by the Committee of Ministers on 28 May 2003, at the 840th meeting of the Ministers' Deputies.

173. Recommendation No. R (99) 1, op. cit. (note 171).

174. Recommendation CM/Rec(2007)3, op. cit. (note 170).

175. Recommendation No. R (99) 1 and Recommendation CM/Rec(2007)2, op. cit. (note 171).

176. Recommendation No. R (99) 1 and Recommendation CM/Rec(2007)2, op. cit. (note 171).

must ensure that the day-to-day management including the editorial responsibility for programme schedules and the content of programmes is a matter decided entirely by the broadcasters themselves. They should adopt appropriate structures such as pluralistic internal boards or other independent bodies,[177] ensuring that people with clear party political affiliations do not hold senior management positions within PSM.[178] In the *Manole* case, the Court further held that the state has a duty to ensure that the public has access through television and radio to impartial and accurate information and a range of opinions and comments, reflecting the diversity of political outlook within the country;[179]

– ensure sufficient and sustained funding of PSM from various sources.[180] At the 4th European Ministerial Conference on Mass Media Policy the member states of the Council of Europe undertook to maintain and, where necessary, establish an appropriate and secure funding framework which guarantees public service broadcasters the means necessary to accomplish their duties.[181]

As noted above, the human rights approach to PSM shall identify the rights holders and duty bearers. In this respect, PSM are not only rights holders. The Council of Europe standards-setting instruments define specific obligations for them. PSM should:

– fulfil their mandate and act in accordance with the law, like all public institutions;

– create and distribute content without interference by public authorities and private interest groups (institutional independence).

---

177. See Prague Resolution No. 1, "The future of public service broadcasting", adopted at the 4th European Ministerial Conference on Mass Media Policy (Prague, 7-8 December 1994) and Recommendation No. R (99) 1, op. cit. (note 171).
178. Resolution 1636 (2008) on indicators for media in a democracy, adopted by the Parliamentary Assembly on 3 October 2008, paragraph 8.20.
179. *Manole and Others v. Moldova*, Appl. No. 13936/02, judgment of 17 September 2009, paragraph 100.
180. Recommendation No. R (99) 1 and Recommendation CM/Rec(2007)2, op. cit. (note 171).
181. Prague Resolution No. 1, op. cit. (note 177).

Resolution 1636 (2008) states that public service broadcasters should establish in-house codes of conduct for journalistic work and editorial independence from political influence;[182]

- ensure accountability through regular evaluation and review of activities, as emphasised by Recommendation CM/Rec(2007)3,[183] in order to ensure that all groups in the audience are adequately served;[184] and

- be open to the public, through the introduction of forms of public consultation, as stated in Recommendation CM/Rec(2007)2.[185] This may include the creation of advisory structures, reflecting public diversity, to ensure programming policy meets public requirements.

Accountability

PSM accountability regimes are normally part of the PSM legal framework. The legal framework specifies the bodies to which the PSM institutions are responsible. Bodies such as parliaments may have formal relationships with PSM, while others – such as PSM staff, civil society organisations or audience councils – have informal relationships with PSM.

PSM should be held accountable for their remit in the first place. But they should also be accountable for administrative operability and financial efficiency. For example, where PSM decide to commission work from independent market players, they should be held accountable for the outcomes.

Normally, the legal framework requires PSM to report on their activities to parliaments. PSM can undergo audit processes too. PSM frameworks set out timetables for annual reports and other audits.

---

182. Resolution 1636 (2008), op. cit. (note 178), paragraph 8.21.
183. Recommendation CM/Rec(2007)3, op. cit. (note 170).
184. Recommendation CM/Rec(2007)3, op. cit. (note 170), Principle No. 6.
185. Recommendation CM/Rec(2007)2, op. cit. (note 171).

Parallel to parliaments, the public can hold PSM institutions accountable through public representatives sitting on a supervisory board. In addition, institutions akin to the ombudsman, audience councils and complaints procedures for breaches of codes of practice can hold PSM accountable for their programming.

Several examples illustrate such institutional arrangements and policies. In Portugal, a listener and viewer Ombudsman is nominated by the Radio and Television Board. In Spain, an Ombudsman for listeners, viewers and media interactive service users is nominated by the president of the Radio Television Corporation (RTVE). The ombudsmen in both countries respond and mediate in the public's name and prepare reports on PSM performance.[186]

The Audience Council of the Öesterreichischer Rundfunk in Austria "safeguard[s] the interests of the listeners and viewers". Its 35 members are made up of representatives from a wide-cross section of civil society organisations from church groups to academics.[187]

In the United Kingdom, viewers can make complaints through the website of the British Broadcasting Corporation (BBC). The BBC Editorial Complaints Unit deals with serious complaints about breaches of the BBC's editorial standards. If complainants are not satisfied by its findings, they can appeal to the Governors' Programme Complaints Committee. For the most serious upheld complaints, an apology or correction from the BBC may be published online or on air.[188]

According to the Council of Europe's declaration on the guarantee of the independence of public service broadcasting in the member

---

186. Nino Conde, PSM ombudsman, "Responsiveness and Accountability", paper presented during the consultation meeting of the Ad hoc Advisory Group on Public Service Media Governance, Strasbourg, 17 and 18 September 2009.
187. See: Federal Act on the Austrian Broadcasting Corporation (ORF Act), Federal Law Gazette No. 379/1984 as amended by Federal Law Gazette I No. 83/2001, available at www.ris.bka.gv.at/Dokumente/Erv/ERV_1984_379/ERV_1984_379.html.
188. BBC Complaints/Editorial Complaints Unit rulings, available at www.bbc.co.uk/complaints/ecu.

states,[189] PSM is "relatively" open and transparent in most states. The declaration, however, notes that in some cases there is insufficient openness, transparency and accountability. Furthermore, in some countries annual reports to national parliaments are rarely the subject of examination or real debate. This may be the result of inexperience in holding PSM publicly accountable or due to a perception that the parliament has a weaker supervisory function if PSM's funding comes from advertisements or licence fees. Whatever the reasons, deficiencies in PSM's accountability affect the public's trust, and lead to alienation of viewers and listeners.

Participation

In the past, many public service broadcasting institutions have kept the public at a distance; governments and politicians were their preferred partners. Because of this lack of dialogue, many viewers, civil society organisations and private media players are indifferent towards or feel alienated by PSM systems. For example, a study established that in December 2007, 72% of the British population had never contacted a news organisation on any platform.[190]

The present social environment, characterised by the informal, participatory and democratic culture of the Internet and the information and communication technologies, challenges the current PSM model. It demands that PSM be responsive and open to partnership with public and private media players as well as being transparent in its decision making. Both PSM legislation and culture should address this demand.

Recommendation Rec(2007)3 on the remit of PSM in the information society[191] calls for PSM to make use of user-generated content

---

189. Declaration of the Committee of Ministers on the guarantee of the independence of public service broadcasting in the member states, adopted on 27 September 2006 at the 974th meeting of the Ministers' Deputies.
190. Claire Wardle, "User generated content and public service broadcasting", available at http://clairewardle.com/2010/05/19/user-generated-content-and-public-service-broadcasting.
191. Recommendation CM/Rec(2007)3, op. cit. (note 170).

and other participatory schemes in order to involve the younger generation in active forms of communication.[192] It is pointed out that PSM should themselves enhance their dialogue with the general public, particularly by using new interactive services.[193] Recommendation CM/Rec(2007)2 on media pluralism and the diversity of media content calls on member states to invite PSM "to envisage the introduction of forms of consultation with the public, which may include the creation of advisory structures, where appropriate reflecting the public in its diversity, so as to reflect in their programming policy the wishes and requirements of the public."[194]

The need for more democratic and participatory governance of PSM has already been identified in some states. For example, during the 2010 UK election campaign, senior Labour cabinet members David Miliband and Tessa Jowell proposed that the BBC be transformed into a co-operative to give licence fee payers a "democratic voice" and make it more accountable. Their argument was that the BBC is owned by the British public and therefore ordinary members of the public should have a real say in how it is run. Miliband and Jowell proposed that the majority of BBC Trust be elected by members' councils representing BBC viewers.

Greater levels of democracy and participation in PSM can be achieved by enabling individuals to:

- give feedback through correspondence with programme creators: it has become normal practice in many countries for programme presenters to invite the audience to write to them by SMS or Twitter, for example;

- participate in online discussions related to programme topics: this option is similar to the first one and is appropriate in cases where the programme has a website or a blog on which viewers can publish their views about the programme;

---

192. Recommendation CM/Rec(2007)3, op. cit. (note 170), Principle No. 5.
193. Recommendation CM/Rec(2007)3, op. cit. (note 170), Principle No. 18.
194. Recommendation CM/Rec(2007)2, op. cit. (note 171).

- access airtime with user-generated content: for example, Channel 4 allows users to upload and view their own documentaries;
- participate in PSM management and formulation of policy: opportunities for this are created through PSM or broadcasting regulators' websites or blogs.

For private media players, PSM democratisation means developing fruitful and co-operative relationships with PSM. Outsourcing some of the content production to independent, private media companies is one way of opening up formerly closed PSM companies and at the same time giving the private sector access to public support as part of a business policy.

Non-discrimination

The rights-based approach to PSM demands that PSM institutions be governed by the principle of equality and freedom from discrimination. At the same time particular focus should be given to the status of vulnerable groups, such as minorities, indigenous peoples and persons with disabilities.

Council of Europe Recommendation No. R (97) 21 on the media and the promotion of a culture of tolerance[195] recognised that "the media can make a positive contribution to the fight against intolerance, especially where they foster a culture of understanding between different ethnic, cultural and religious groups in society." Referring to states' commitment to equality and the prohibition of discrimination on any grounds, the recommendation emphasises the need for training, standard-setting (especially through codes of conduct) and access for minority groups to media. Public service broadcasters are advised to consider:

- making adequate provision for programme services, including those at popular viewing times, which help to promote the

---

195. Recommendation No. R (97) 21 of the Committee of Ministers on the media and the promotion of a culture of tolerance, adopted on 30 October 1997 at the 607th meeting of the Ministers' Deputies.

integration of all individuals, groups and communities as well as proportionate amounts of airtime for the various ethnic, religious and other communities;

- developing a multicultural approach to programme content so as to avoid programmes which present society in mono-cultural and mono-linguistic terms;

- promoting a multicultural approach in programmes which are specifically geared to children and young people so as to enable them to grow up with the understanding that cultural, religious and ethnic differences are a natural and positive element of society;

- developing arrangements for sharing, at the regional, national or European level, programme material which has proven its value in mobilising public opinion against intolerance and improving community relations in multi-ethnic and multicultural societies.

Furthermore, Recommendation CM/Rec(2007)3 on the remit of the PSM in the information society[196] calls on Council of Europe member states to, *inter alia*, offer universal access to PSM for all individuals and social groups, including minority and disadvantaged groups, through a range of technologies. It stipulates that:

> *Public service media should integrate all communities, social groups and generations, including minority groups, young people, old persons, the most disadvantaged social categories, persons with disabilities, while respecting their different identities and needs. In this context, attention should be paid to the content created by and for such groups, and to their access to, and presence and portrayal in, public service media. Due attention should be also paid to gender equality issues.[197]*

The 2005 UNESCO Convention on the Protection and Promotion of the Diversity of Cultural Expressions,[198] further underpins nation states' rights to take measures aimed at enhancing the diversity of the media, including through public service broadcasting. The convention

---

196. Recommendation CM/Rec(2007)3, op. cit. (note 170).
197. Recommendation CM/Rec(2007)3, Section 8, op. cit. (note 170).
198. Adopted on 20 October 2005, entered into force on 18 March 2007.

emphasises that cultural diversity – flourishing within a framework of democracy, tolerance, social justice and mutual respect among peoples and cultures – is indispensable for peace and security at local, national and international levels.

A number of broadcasting laws in Europe include the obligation to promote equality and fight discrimination. In addition, several codes of conducts or ethical codes also impose respect for equality and protection of minorities, including:

- the French Law of 30 September 1986, defining the mission of public services. It states that public service broadcasters must implement actions in favour of social cohesion and cultural diversity, combat discrimination, and propose programmes reflecting the diversity of French society;[199]

- the Spanish Law No. 17/2006, regulating national public service broadcasting. This requires the Corporation RTVE, which manages national public service broadcasting, to encourage the integration of minorities and social groups with special needs, preserve gender equality, protect the rights of children and promote the protection of the environment. The *Mandato-Marco* of December 2007, a framework agreement that specifies the public service remit of RTVE, refers to "the plurality of the society which must be reflected without any discrimination"[200] and states that RTVE shall "offer contents related to minorities, integration of immigrants and religious beliefs; it will also broadcast the different cultural expressions, Spanish or foreign, in national and international scope";

- the legal obligation of the public broadcaster in Cyprus to provide an output for all citizens with respect to their age, gender, colour, belief, religion, political or other opinions, national, ethnic or social origin, and membership of any minority;

---

199. The Law of 30 September 1986, Article 43-11.
200. Article 11 of Mandato-Marco, cited in Institut für Europäisches Medienrecht (2009), *Public service media according to constitutional jurisprudence*, EMR, Saarbrücken/Brüssel, see: www.ebu.ch/CMSimages/en/leg_EMR_PSM_study_tcm6-67510.pdf.

–   the Television Act of Portugal, which requires public service broadcasters to promote a culture of tolerance. Public service broadcast operators are obliged to provide pluralistic programming that takes into account minority interests and promotes cultural diversity. They must broadcast culture, education and information programmes aiming at specific audiences, including the immigrant communities established in Portugal.

Focus on promotion of non-discrimination and equality should therefore be strengthened in the development of PSM policies. Specifically, PSM should prioritise their initiatives to those groups suffering the greatest discrimination and disadvantage. PSM institutions should also make their content available in accessible formats and minority languages.

Empowerment

Individuals, groups and legal entities are not empowered by human and legal rights unless there are mechanisms they can use to enforce their rights. In order to be empowered by their rights, PSM and other rights holders should be able to hold the state accountable for the fulfilment of its obligations and commitment with respect to PSM. At the same time PSM should be accountable to the viewers and listeners for the fulfilment of their obligations. Below we examine how state and PSM institutional obligations and commitments relating to PSM can be enforced.

Enforcement of state human rights obligations

The ECHR requires that victims or potential victims of human rights violations, whether persons or legal entities, have legal remedies at the national level. The rights proclaimed in the ECHR are either incorporated into domestic law or victims can have direct recourse to them. Proceedings against state or judicial acts infringing upon the right to freedom of expression of journalists, PSM or the general public can be brought to courts or other bodies competent to enforce human rights. If courts find that an act of a public authority is unlawful because of a conflict with a Convention right, they can grant such relief or remedy or make such order within their powers as they consider just and appropriate.

At the European level the Court safeguards the implementation of the rights guaranteed by the ECHR, acting on individual or state complaints. Likewise, the European Committee of Social Rights monitors compliance in the member states to the European Social Charter and can examine collective complaints. The Committee of Ministers of the Council of Europe is responsible for ensuring that the Court's judgments are enforced. It also monitors the state of human rights and exerts pressure upon governments which violate them. PACE debates human rights issues and adopts resolutions and recommendations for member states concerning specific and broader issues relating to the situation of human rights in Europe. For example, in 1999 PACE recommended that the Committee of Ministers "monitor closely the state of freedom of the press in European member and non-member countries so as to exert moral and political pressure upon governments which violate freedom of expression and defend and protect journalists who are victims of such violations."[201]

The Commissioner for Human Rights promotes education in, awareness of and respect for human rights in the member states of the Council of Europe. He issues reports, recommendations and opinions[202] based on information gathered during country visits and dialogue with national institutions. He publishes issue papers[203]

201. Recommendation 1407 (1999) on media and democratic culture, adopted by the Parliamentary Assembly of the Council of Europe on 29 April 1999.
202. See: "Opinion of the Commissioner for Human Rights on Hungary's media legislation in light of Council of Europe standards on freedom of the media", CommDH(2011)10, Strasbourg, 25 February 2011.
203. See: "Ethical journalism and human rights", Issue discussion paper commissioned and published by Thomas Hammarberg, CommDH(2011)40.

and opinions[204] that identify thematic concerns and propose solutions. In this regard, the Commissioner has undertaken work on media freedom and adopted positions that contain many important recommendations.[205]

The Organization for Security and Co-operation (OSCE) in Europe has mandated its Representative on Freedom of the Media to observe relevant media development in participating states. The Representative should also advocate and promote full compliance with OSCE principles and commitments regarding freedom of expression and free media. The Representative concentrates on rapid response to serious non-compliance with these principles, contacting the participating state and the parties concerned, assessing the facts, assisting the participating state and contributing to the resolution of the problem. To achieve her mandate, the OSCE Representative on Freedom of the Media collects information on the situation of the media, to be forwarded to the Permanent Council of the OSCE and recommending further action where appropriate.

Enforcement of state obligations and commitments concerning PSM

The non-binding nature of international agreements and standard-setting instruments relating to PSM means that even if a government has made a commitment with respect to PSM, there is no enforcement mechanism to hold it responsible for failures to embed its commitments in law and media policies. This is why the roles of PSM and international monitoring organisations such as the Council of Europe are crucial to exposing violations and contraventions of international guidelines and commitments.

---

204. See Thomas Hammarberg, "Media diversity: a core element of true democracy", Viewpoint, 1 October 2007; "Investigative journalists and whistle-blowers must be protected", Viewpoint, 17 September 2007; "Do not criminalize critical remarks against religion", Viewpoint, 11 June 2007.
205. See: Positions on Freedom of the Media. Position Paper from the Council of Europe Commissioner for Human Rights, CommDH/PositionPaper(2010)2, Strasbourg, 3 May 2010.

The Committee of Ministers adopts standard-setting instruments on PSM and monitors their implementation. The assessment of the implementation is carried out by the Steering Committee on the Mass Media, which conducts assessments of the implementation by member states of non-binding documents prepared under its authority. Expert committees meet under its general auspices to discuss PSM issues.

PACE has considered issues related to PSM. In 2004, it adopted a recommendation concerning public service broadcasting.[206] The PACE Committee on Culture, Science and Education and its Sub-Committee on the Media hears reports about the situation of media freedom in Europe, including PSM, and drafts recommendations.[207]

The Commissioner for Human Rights also looks into the situation of the PSM. In 2011, the Commissioner criticised the new media legislation in Hungary, including the placement of the PSM under government control.[208] Since 2001 the Rapporteur on Media Freedom has monitored situation in Europe, and brought serious threats to the attention of the Committee on Culture, Science and Education, including information about the PSM situation.[209]

How a rights-based approach can improve PSM

Figure 1 summarises the stakeholders within PSM and their current approaches.

---

206. See Recommendation 1641 (2004) on public service broadcasting, adopted by the Assembly on 27 January 2004.
207. For example: Public service broadcasting. Report, Committee on Culture, Science and Education, Rapporteur: Mr Paschal Mooney, Ireland, Liberal, Democratic and Reformer's Group, Doc. 10029, 12 January 2004.
208. CommDH(2011)10, op. cit. (note 202).
209. Respect for media freedom. Report by Committee on Culture, Science and Education, Rapporteur: Mr Andrew McIntosh, United Kingdom, Socialist Group, Doc. 12102, 6 January 2010.

Figure 1: PSM stakeholder concerns

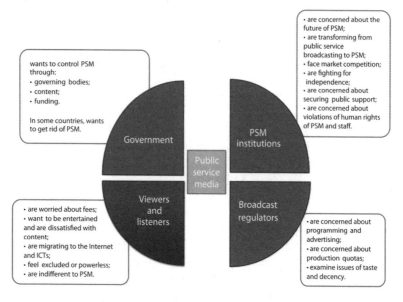

wants to control PSM through:
• governing bodies;
• content;
• funding.

In some countries, wants to get rid of PSM.

• are concerned about the future of PSM;
• are transforming from public service broadcasting to PSM;
• face market competition;
• are fighting for independence;
• are concerned about securing public support;
• are concerned about violations of human rights of PSM and staff.

Government

PSM institutions

Public service media

Viewers and listeners

Broadcast regulators

• are worried about fees;
• want to be entertained and are dissatisfied with content;
• are migrating to the Internet and ICTs;
• feel excluded or powerless;
• are indifferent to PSM.

• are concerned about programming and advertising;
• are concerned about production quotas;
• examine issues of taste and decency.

The rights-based approach to PSM in Figure 2 illustrates how this configuration could change.

The rights-based approach to PSM would provide a transformative solution to the current challenges faced by PSM institutions. Holding governments accountable for their duties with respect to PSM will benefit the transformation process from public service broadcasting to PSM inasmuch as the latter requires legislative changes and financial support. At the same time the focus on PSM transparency and accountability will secure PSM independence from the government and private actors.

Increased public participation in PSM content production and governance will result in new ideas and better leadership and as a result will improve PSM performance. PSM policies which take account of public participation, inclusiveness and non-discrimination will strengthen the role of PSM in fostering democracy and will increase public support for PSM.

Figure 2: PSM stakeholders in rights-based approach

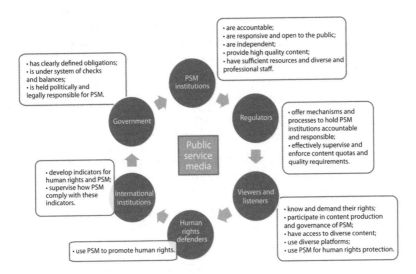

Initiatives to improve public service media in Europe

At present, there are a number of initiatives, at both the regional and national levels, which aim to improve various aspects of PSM. These initiatives basically focus on the functions of PSM in the digital era, PSM governance and the independence of PSM.

At the European level, the Council of Europe has formed an Ad hoc Advisory Group on Public Service Media Governance (MC-S-PG). In April 2011, the MC-S-PG published the draft declaration of the Committee of Ministers on public service media governance,[210] which discusses opportunities and challenges for PSM in the "new digital

---

210. Draft declaration of the Committee of Ministers on public service media governance, Strasbourg, 29 April 2011; available at www.coe.int/t/dghl/standardsetting/media/MC-S-PG/MC-S-PG_2011_002rev4%20Draft%20declaration%20of%20the%20Committee%20of%20Ministers%20on%20public%20service%20media%20governance.pdf.

media" environment. The draft emphasises the need for appropriate systems of governance in order to meet these challenges and to take full advantage of new opportunities. The MC-S-PG also adopted a draft recommendation of the Committee of Ministers on public service media governance,[211] which includes a number of recommendations that member states:

- recognise the need for PSM to develop within a sustainable governance framework which secures both the necessary editorial independence and public accountability;

- further strengthen and, where necessary, enhance the appropriate legal and financial environment, thereby guaranteeing the independence and sustainable development of PSM, empowering them to take up the challenges of technological progress and editorial competition;

- encourage PSM and provide them with the necessary resources and tools to review and develop their internal and external governance arrangements, at whatever stage of maturity they are at, drawing inspiration from the appended guiding principles;

- encourage PSM to co-operate actively on a pan-European scale and to exchange best practices and best content in order to create a vibrant European public sphere and foster democratic citizenship within wider Europe;

- ensure the largest possible distribution of the appended guiding principles, which are designed to allow PSM to reinforce their essential position in the media system and improve their functioning in the digital environment in order to fulfil their democratic mission.

---

211. Draft recommendation of the Committee of Ministers on public service media governance, Strasbourg, 29 April 2011; available at www.coe.int/t/dghl/standardsetting/media/MC-S-PG/MC-S-PG_2011_003rev4%20Draft%20recommendation%20of%20the%20Committee%20of%20Ministers%20on%20public%20service%20media%20governance.pdf.

At EU level, in November 2010, the European Parliament passed a new resolution on public service broadcasting in the digital era.[212] The resolution acknowledges the importance of the Council of Europe's recommendations and declarations, which have been agreed upon by all the EU member states and lay down European standards relating to freedom of expression, press freedom, media pluralism and the independence, organisation, remit and funding of PSM, particularly in the information society, thereby safeguarding the credibility of public service broadcasting. *Inter alia*, the resolution calls on member states to ensure that there are sufficient resources to enable public service broadcasters to take advantage of the new digital technologies and to secure the benefits of modern audiovisual services for the general public. It also calls for PSM to be structured in such a way as to offer attractive, quality online content in order to reach young people who access the media almost exclusively via the Internet. The member states are also asked to adequately address the issue of underfunding of public service broadcasters, bearing in mind particularly the specific remit of the public media to be accessible to the greatest possible number of viewers and listeners on all new media platforms.

At national level, states and PSM institutions undertake a number of initiatives both to improve PSM governance and to expand their services to make them more participatory and inclusive. For example in France, in a web on-demand radio station, ARTE Radio, the Franco-German PSM operator ARTE uses the Créative Commons licensing approach to all content. The enterprise is an open platform where listeners submit material which is posted on the site. ARTE offers the space and then content is posted, building a community partnership between user-generated content and ARTE Radio's own work and production. In Germany, ARD.de offers a specific online service based on the Internet presence of the nine public service broadcasters, and ZDF offers a programme allowing children to put questions

---

212. The European Parliament resolution of 25 November 2010 on "Public service broadcasting in the digital era: The future of the dual system", 2010/2028(INI); available at www.europarl.europa.eu/RegData/seance_pleniere/textes_adoptes/ provisoire/2010/11-25/0438/P7_TA-PROV(2010)0438_EN.pdf.

to politicians. The "Today" programme of BBC Radio 4 links radio and the Internet and gives listeners the opportunity to influence the programme's content and approach by asking questions and providing input. The BBC's Action Network provides advice and tools to those who want to run campaigns on largely local concerns. In Denmark, the DR daily radio programme "Poul Friis" on P1 involves citizens' participation via public debates combining radio or TV shows with Internet debate and "Dogworld", where young people between 11 and 17 years of age learn democracy through games. On Radio Sweden, online services to promote diversity include web news offered in 11 different languages through the international section of the site, web-radio channels in Finnish and Sami for these minority groups (although some of these services were cut in the last year), and Ring P1 – a forum where people can call in to the radio programme.[213]

Recommendations and conclusions

To summarise, PSM can be improved by:

- developing indicators for a rights-based approach to PSM;
- conducting studies on how PSM systems in Europe meet these criteria, and proposing recommendations for improvement and full incorporation of a rights-based approach to the existing systems;
- advocacy to ensure that human rights are taken into account in PSM policies;
- encouraging regulators to supervise and enforce the human rights aspects of the PSM remit;
- encouraging civil society and human rights defenders to promote awareness on public values for which PSM stand and to use PSM to strengthen human rights protection.

---

213. For details of these initiatives, see "Public service media governance: Looking to the future", Media and Information Society Division, Directorate General of Human Rights and Legal Affairs, Council of Europe, April 2009; available at www.coe.int/t/dghl/standardsetting/media/doc/PSMgovernance_en.pdf.

Council of Europe member states are in particular encouraged to:

- maintain and support PSM as a public good needed for human rights, equality, empowerment and citizens' participation in public life;
- ensure that human rights are taken into account in PSM legislation and policies;
- fulfil their obligations to PSM as defined by Council of Europe recommendations and resolutions and the case law of the Court;
- create mechanisms that allow viewers and listeners to hold PSM accountable and responsible;
- use human rights protection to set the PSM remit.

Conclusions

Given the developments and challenges discussed in this chapter, we believe there is a pressing need to urge states and civil society actors to intensify their efforts to support PSM and to provide them with guidance in their approach.

The future of PSM has been questioned, but PSM institutions will continue to operate in Europe because people care about good quality media, and value PSM commitment to accurate, unbiased reporting. Moreover, the significant investments and infrastructure for operation of PSM demand transformative as opposed to revolutionary solutions. We believe that the rights-based approach to PSM policy can offer such transformative solutions.

Drawing on human rights principles, this approach can ensure accountability, participation, non-discrimination and empowerment in the field of PSM. The rights-based approach demands the establishment of mechanisms to ensure transparency and accountability within government and PSM institutions. It can improve PSM image and performance by advocating interactive and inclusive systems of governance and programme policies. The rights-based approach to PSM can ensure that viewers and listeners have access to diverse content addressing their individual and group interests, and demands that PSM promote human rights.

Chapter 6:
Social media and human rights

Douwe Korff, Professor of International Law, London
Metropolitan University
Ian Brown, Senior Research Fellow, Oxford Internet Institute,
University of Oxford

Freedom of expression on the Internet is a
fundamental freedom of our age. Together with
Internet privacy, it is vital to our freedoms to
communicate and associate, and to collectively
determine how our societies should be run.

*A man taking pictures with his mobile phone in Tahrir Square, Cairo, 1 February 2011,
during the upheavals in Egypt. Photo courtesy of Ahmad Hammoud.*

Summary

This chapter focuses on the human rights issues raised by the use of online social media for political activism. Blogs, video and social networking sites have become a key forum for political debate and organisation – so much so that they have provoked counter-responses from some repressive states.

Section one of this chapter describes these counter-measures. Some states have adopted Internet blocking, filtering or takedown procedures or Internet surveillance (including compulsory data retention), or even shut down national networks, in attempts to restrain users' freedoms. And in many otherwise democratic countries, the use of measures such as blocking and monitoring still leaves much to be desired in terms of human rights.

Section two examines the legal issues raised by such counter-measures, and suggests how human rights protections could be improved. We describe the body of principles that aims to orient legislation in Council of Europe member states. Its sources include the European Convention on Human Rights (ECHR) and associated case law – developed primarily for the offline world; other conventions and resolutions, including the Council of Europe Convention on Cybercrime; and an emerging body of Internet governance principles.

Our conclusions indicate three areas that require solutions: a weakness in the European Court of Human Rights' doctrine of discretion for individual states; the need to bolster the role of private sector intermediaries with requirements for them to defend their users' Internet freedoms; and the demands of the rule of law. We propose solutions as a basis for further discussion of what are undoubtedly serious challenges.

Introduction

The Internet and social media have become increasingly important in political activity. Blogging, video-sharing and tweeting were crucial in the political events in North Africa and the Middle East in 2011. They are important to human rights defenders everywhere. But the use of these new technologies to assert old freedoms has been met with repression by some governments.

A recent study of 37 countries by Freedom House cites increasing website blocking and filtering, content manipulation, attacks on and imprisonment of bloggers, punishment of ordinary users, cyber attacks and coercion of website owners to remove content, in attempts by authoritarian states to reduce political opposition. It suggests that Internet restrictions around the globe are partly a response to the exploding popularity, and significant role in political and social activism, of sites like Facebook, YouTube and Twitter. Governments consistently or temporarily closed down such sites in 12 of the countries studied, including Egypt and Tunisia where democracy advocates relied heavily on Facebook to mobilise supporters and organise mass rallies.[214]

Of the various means of suppressing communication by Internet, the most extreme have involved simply cutting off all Internet access (Egypt, January 2011, and Syria at the time of writing),[215] or even creating a completely state-controlled mini-Net (apparently planned by Iran).[216] In other cases, such as Bahrain, governments have used their control over local Internet structure to deliberately slow down connection speeds, in particular at newspaper offices, hotels and homes. Thailand, Burma, China and Iran have tried to manipulate online discussions through organised pro-state submissions. China has pressured search engines to distort search results. In several countries, bloggers and Internet activists have been subjected to threats and physical attack. Following riots in several British cities, the government proposed taking powers to shut down social networking

214. Kelly S. and Cook S. (eds) (2011), *Freedom on the Net 2011: A global assessment of Internet and digital media*, Freedom House, Washington, DC; see: www.freedomhouse. org/uploads/fotn/2011/FOTN2011.pdf.
215. "Syrian Internet shutdown", Renesys blog, 3 June 2011, see: www.renesys.com/ blog/2011/06/syrian-internet-shutdown.shtml.
216. "Iran vows to unplug Internet", *Wall Street Journal Online*, 28 May 2011, quotes Iran's head of economic affairs as saying the aim is to create "a genuinely halal network, aimed at Muslims on an ethical and moral level", largely detached from the worldwide web: http://online.wsj.com/article/SB10001424052748704889404576277391449002016.html.

sites during future recurrences. This last proposal was withdrawn after widespread public criticism (but approval from official Chinese media).

Of the eight Council of Europe member states covered by the Freedom House study, four were ranked "Free" in terms of Internet freedom – Estonia, Germany, Italy and the United Kingdom (though this did not mean there were no issues), and four – Azerbaijan, Georgia, Russia and Turkey – were ranked "Partially Free", meaning they have significant Internet freedom problems.

An interactive "Internet in Europe" map produced by the media innovation group OWNI reveals serious issues throughout the European region, including the four countries ranked "Free" by Freedom House.[217] In 7 of the 24 European countries on which information was available – Belgium, France, Italy, Romania, Spain, Denmark and Sweden – OWNI judged Internet filtering to be "rampant and problematic: (no judge involved in the process, lack of transparency concerning who [that is, what] is targeted, etc.)".

Measures that states use to interfere with Internet freedoms, and their limitations

Blocking

The main aim of blocking is to prevent specific Internet content from reaching a final user, by software or hardware that reviews communications and decides on the basis of pre-set criteria whether to prevent receipt. It does not affect the target material. A common aim

---

217. The map rates countries in six categories: intellectual property (enforcement of protected content); data retention (transposition of the EC Data Retention Directive); mobile (denial of certain functionalities); filtering (including blocking of child pornography and online gambling sites); support for ACTA (the Anti-Counterfeiting Trade Agreement); and copyright (level of piracy). We use the ranking for filtering (though the map only looks at non-political filtering), because the main issue here is one of process rather than of what is being filtered. The maps for filtering and data retention are at: http://owni.fr/2011/05/25/carte-internet-europe-regulation-filtrage-copyright-droit-liberte-utilisateurs.

is blocking images of child abuse; however, this does not obliterate the images, nor remove them from the Internet. A more effective response would be to remove images from the Internet, criminally investigate producers and save children from such situations. Blocking does none of that.[218] In human rights law, this problem relates to the legal criterion of whether it is effective, and thus "proportional".

Blocking is a broad term: not all types are equally effective, nor legally equivalent. The term may suggest that Internet blocking is easy – like throwing a switch – but the capabilities of the technologies are complex and can often be easily bypassed.[219] Blocking is also subject to "false positives" (blocking of sites with no prohibited material) and "false negatives" (when sites with prohibited material slip through a filter).[220] All blocking technologies reviewed in an Open Society Institute study were flawed in terms of over- or under-blocking. Most were easy to circumvent; all could be circumvented without much effort by determined people.[221] This is good news for political activists

---

218. Callanan C. et al. (2009), "Internet blocking: balancing cybercrime responses in democratic societies", Aconite/OSI, full report and summary at: www.aconite.com/sites/default/files/Internet_blocking_and_Democracy.pdf; www.aconite.com/sites/default/files/Internet_Blocking_and_Democracy_Exec_Summary.pdf. Blocking activities of selected states have been extensively analysed by others, including one of the authors. See for instance, Brown I. (2008), "Internet filtering – be careful what you ask for", Kirca S. and Hanson L. (eds) *Freedom and prejudice: Approaches to media and culture*, Bahcesehir University Press, Istanbul.

219. Chapter 5 of the report summarises the complex range of technology issues, and a brief discussion of the various approaches (target-based, decision-maker-based, etc.) is in the Executive Summary, and Brown (2008), ibid.

220. For examples of "over-blocking" and its causes see Brown (2008), ibid – including Pennsylvania's Internet filtering law, struck down in 2004 partially because of over-blocking: the blocking of 400 sites had prevented access to over 1.1 million others, while being easily circumvented. The Court found no evidence that the Act "reduced child exploitation or abuse" (*CDT v. Pappert*, 2004).

221. An overview of evasion technologies (proxy servers, "tunnelling", "hosting or URL rotation", botnets, evading DNS-based filters) is on pp. 18-19 of the Executive Summary of Callanan et al. (2009), op. cit. (note 218) – with a useful chart (p. 17) indicating the characteristics of the various blocking strategies discussed: the likelihood of over- and under-blocking; the resources and maintenance effort required for each; and the intrusiveness in terms of deep-packet inspection (DPI) requirements.

in repressive countries, but bad news for states, officials and private entities hoping to use blocking to stop dissemination of child abuse images or hate speech.[222]

In all the countries studied, Freedom House found arbitrariness and opacity surrounding decisions to block content: "in most non-democratic settings there is little government effort to inform the public what content is censored and why." The authorities often avoid confirming that a website has been blocked and instead remain silent or cite technical problems: "even in more transparent, democratic environments, censorship decisions are often made by private entities and without public discussion, and appeals processes may be onerous, little known, or non-existent".[223]

Thus, no one knows what is on the blocking lists of "partially free" Azerbaijan, Georgia, Russia or Turkey. In these and other European countries, the criteria for blocking are totally unclear. The application of blocking is unforeseeable, and effectively unchallengeable.

Once blocking lists are introduced, they can grow. There have been attempts to block sites containing not only hate speech and advocacy of terrorism, but also political debate, information on minority rights, alleged defamation, purported copyright infringement – even the "sacred texts" of Scientology.[224]

Censorship by pressure

Government officials increasingly contact authors or websites to apply pressure for content to be removed, with threats of legal action, withdrawal of contracts or licences and outright bans – even where companies are based in overseas jurisdictions. A "word in the ear" of a senior executive can be as effective.[225] After all, companies are

---

222. See: Clayton R., "Failures in a hybrid content blocking system", Proceedings of the 5th Workshop on Privacy Enhancing Technologies, Dubrovnik, May 2005, available at: www.cl.cam.ac.uk/~rnc1/cleanfeed.pdf.

223. Kelly and Cook (2011), op. cit. (note 214), pp. 4-5.

224. Brown (2008), op. cit. (note 218).

225. Anderson M., "A sneak peek at a fractured web", Wired News, November 13, 2006, at: www.wired.com/news/technology/0,72104-0.html.

generally seeking to maximise profit; that is their *raison d'être*, not the protection of free speech.

Governments also encourage their supporters to complain to hosting companies about user-generated content. YouTube and Facebook have removed or disabled activist accounts in China, Egypt, Ethiopia, Mexico and Tunisia following such complaints.[226]

These pressures raise human rights questions – including the issue of whether companies should have obligations to resist pressure as a means of safeguarding their users' human rights.[227]

Restrictive measures across country boundaries

Two methods are used to reach across country boundaries to restrict information flow:

The first is direct action (for instance, prosecution) by a state against individuals or companies acting through sites hosted in another state, which has significant implications in human rights law.[228] Examples (discussed in section two) include the conviction by a British court of a French national resident in the United Kingdom (*Perrin*), who owned and operated a US-based website, and an order by a French court against (US-based) Yahoo! for allowing the offer of items deemed illegal in France to French citizens, on a US-based website.

Secondly, governments may threaten foreign companies, even where the related content is not illegal, with serious commercial sanctions for facilitating dissemination. This raises the question of whether private entities that have the technical responsibility for delivering content should have a legal obligation to defend their users' human rights, even in a foreign context.

---

226. Kelly and Cook (2011), op. cit. (note 214), p. 8.

227. Ibid., pp. 7-8.

228. In discussing transnational legal action, we exclude actions by states against their own nationals (or residents) for accessing or disseminating material downloaded from other countries – though this may well breach international human rights law (and if in Europe, the ECHR).

Internet surveillance

The authorities are often interested to know who is trying to access banned material. The famous 1983 *Census* judgment of the German Constitutional Court said:

> A social and legal order in which the citizen can no longer know who knows what about him, and when, and in what situation, is incompatible with the right to informational self-determination.
>
> A person who wonders whether unusual behaviour is noted each time, and thereafter always kept on record, used or disseminated, will try not to come to attention in this way ...
>
> This would ... limit the ... common good, because self-determination is an essential prerequisite for a free and democratic society that is based on the capacity and solidarity of its citizens. [229]

In repressive countries, the purpose of identifying those trying to access banned material may be to target opposition activists. In democracies, such surveillance may easily slip from targeting actual terrorists to those sympathetic to terrorists, or simply those with "extreme" views. For many years, anti-terrorism and emergency legislation has been extended in this way.[230]

The Internet and other modern communication technologies have opened new possibilities for the ubiquitous surveillance of people, on the basis of what they read or discuss, with whom they discuss it, who they "chat" with, what blogs they visit, what online videos they watch or what they upload.

We may think we are free and unobserved when we surf the Internet, chat with friends, send out tweets or upload video clips from our

---

229. BVerfGE Bd. 65, S. 1 ff. (our translation).
230. See, for example, from our own experience: Korff D. (1983), "Aspects of the law regarding freedom of expression in the Federal Republic of Germany", later used (with the author's trial observation report on the case against Haag et al.) in the AI publication "Prosecution for the exercise of the right to freedom of expression in the Federal Republic of Germany", AI Document EUR 23/02/85, London, 1985, or Korff D. (1986), "Criminal-legal restrictions on freedom of expression in Israel and the Occupied Territories", used in an AI Submission to the Israeli Government later that year.

mobile phone. In practice, essentially everything we do or say or watch on the Internet is logged, and in principle available for analysis – unless we take elaborate precautions. If we do, that in itself is likely to flag us up to those watching.[231] This allows repressive states to monitor and link activists, with a view to harassment, arrest and worse. Even in liberal democracies, this has led to the monitoring of peaceful activists.

"Simple" surveillance of communication – not capturing content, but monitoring only who communicates with whom, when, where – can be intrusive. This "social network analysis" is increasingly used in investigation and surveillance by police and state security agencies.[232] Repressive countries can easily use it to note, map and target social networks used for political activism.

Data retention

"Data retention" refers to compulsory retention by communication service providers (including internet service providers, or ISPs) of the communication records of all their clients – beyond the normal (billing) period for keeping data – "just in case" the data might be useful in some future police or secret service enquiry. This ought to be viewed as mass surveillance of citizens without due cause: a fundamental departure from a basic principle of the rule of law.

Under criminal law, repressive measures such as phone secrecy violation, mail opening, searches of premises or people, and arrests are allowed only on the basis of indications that a criminal offence has been committed, and indication of a specific individual's involvement in it. Countries use different terms such as "reasonable suspicion" and "factual indications" but all require at least some basis of indication of illegality before intrusive measures are allowed, and

---

231. Brown I. and Korff D. (2009), "Terrorism and the proportionality of Internet surveillance", *European Journal of Criminology*, 6(2), pp. 119-134.
232. Opening page to: "Revealing links: The power of social network analysis – A new i2 White Paper", Issue 1, May 2010. The rest of the paper provides important further descriptions and illustrations.

correlate the intrusiveness of the measures to the level of real or factual evidence available, and to various procedural safeguards. For example, when evidence is "soft", relatively unobtrusive measures are typically authorised, with relatively light procedural requirements (in an urgent case, perhaps no more than a requirement for an official record and a *post facto* review). More intrusive measures (house searches, arrest, etc.) require strong indications of criminal acts and personal involvement, and authorisation by a court.

Compulsory data retention rides roughshod over this principle. It is an affront to the rule of law, to the very principles that the Council of Europe stand for – and a signal to countries in other parts of the world that such a basic principle can be set aside if deemed inconvenient. This is why it has faced such forceful opposition, and why constitutional and other courts in several European Union (EU) member states have ruled it to be incompatible with fundamental rights.

Even so, the executive and political arms of the EU – the European Commission and the EU Council – have been pressing on with the concept, and are even taking legal enforcement action against several states which have not implemented the EU Data Retention Directive (Directive 2006/24/EC), or which have had to withdraw draft laws implementing it, because they violated the state's national constitution. An evaluation report by the European Commission was rightly dismissed as a "whitewash" by civil liberty and civil society organisations.[233]

As European Digital Rights (EDRi) and other organisations point out, European bodies, including the EU and the Council

---

233. EDRi, 17 April 2011 at: www.edri.org/data-retention-shadow-report. The text of the Data Retention Directive (full title: Directive 2006/24/EC of the European Parliament and of The Council of 15 March 2006 on the retention of data generated or processed in connection with the provision of publicly available electronic communications services or of public communications networks and amending Directive 2002/58/EC) can be found at: http://eur-lex.europa.eu/LexUriServ/LexUriServ.do?uri=OJ:L:2006:105:0054:0063:EN:PDF. The Commission evaluation report is at: http://ec.europa.eu/commission_2010-2014/malmstrom/archive/20110418_data_retention_evaluation_en.pdf; and the full EDRi "shadow evaluation report" is at: www.edri.org/files/shadow_drd_report_110417.pdf.

of Europe, cannot on the one hand object to interference with the rights of online activists in oppressive countries, while on the other hand introduce, and forcefully pursue, the very same kind of measures, with the same absence of control and oversight, against their own populations.

These measures are also in breach of fundamental European human rights – including those in the ECHR and in the Charter of Fundamental Rights of the EU. This is the opinion not only of civil liberty groups, but also of the official EU monitor on this subject, the European Data Protection Supervisor.

Applying human rights and emerging Internet governance standards to political activism and counter-measures on the Internet

Basic legal principles, criteria, interpretation

The interrelated freedoms of communication, expression and association are at the heart of any free, democratic society based on the rule of law. From the relevant articles (8, 10, 11) of the ECHR, the Strasbourg Court has developed standard basic tests to be applied to restrictions placed on these rights, which must:

- be based on "law", that is on legal rules that meet quality requirements of clarity, accessibility and foreseeability;

- serve a legitimate purpose in such a society, that is a "pressing social need";

- be "necessary" to achieve that purpose, that is they must not be disproportionate to the purpose, nor ineffective;

- have an "effective remedy", preferably judicial, if they do not meet these tests.[234]

---

234. See: Harris D. et al. (2009), *Law of the European Convention on Human Rights*, (2nd edn), Chapter 8 (Articles 8-11: General Considerations), Chapter 14 (Article 13: The Right to an Effective Remedy) and Chapter 6 (Article 6: The Right to a Fair Trial). For a simpler overview of these standards, see Korff D., "The standard approach

These standards are expressed in the case law of the Court and other international human rights bodies, such as the Human Rights Committee, which applies the provisions of the International Covenant on Civil and Political Rights (ICCPR).

Application in practice – mitigated by the doctrine of "margin of appreciation"

The Strasbourg Court's famous 1976 *Handyside* judgment, on the banning of the publication in England of the *Little Red Schoolbook* on the grounds that it "corrupted public morals",[235] states a firm principle: freedom of expression is one of the essential foundations of a "democratic society", a basic condition for its progress and for every person's development, applicable (subject to Article 10.2), not only to "information" or "ideas" that are regarded favourably, or as inoffensive or with indifference, but also to those that offend, shock or disturb the state or any sector of the population. The judgment noted: "Such are the demands of that pluralism, tolerance and broadmindedness without which there is no 'democratic society.'"

The *Handyside* judgment, applying this to "protection of morals", qualifies the powerful dictum under Article 10.2, by saying that, since there is no single European conception of morals visible in each state's law, and since local laws on morals change by time and place, state authorities themselves are better placed than an international judge to give an opinion on the exact content of each country's requirements in terms of morals, and whether any restriction on the freedom of expression is "necessary" to meet "a pressing social need". Consequently, the Court considered that Article 10.2 leaves to contracting states a "margin of appreciation".

---

under Articles 8-11 ECHR and Article 2 ECHR", available from: www.coehelp.org/mod/resource/view.php?inpopup=true&id=2130. For details of the application of these principles in the field of freedom of expression, see the Council of Europe Human Rights Handbook on Article 10, available from: www.coehelp.org/file.php/54/resources/Handbooks/art_10_eng.pdf.

235. *Handyside v. the United Kingdom*, Appl. No. 5493/72, judgment of 7 December 1976, paragraph 49.

However, Article 10.2 does not give contracting states unlimited "appreciation". The Court can give a final ruling on whether a restriction or penalty is reconcilable with freedom of expression as protected by Article 10. The margin of appreciation goes "hand in hand with" European supervision, which applies to the aim of the measure challenged, and its "necessity", as well as to the decision applying it. The judgment refers to Article 50 of the ECHR ("decision or ... measure taken by a legal authority or any other authority"), and its own case law.

Since the *Handyside* judgment, the margin of appreciation doctrine has been applied to all substantive articles of the ECHR. It has made the Court's case law somewhat unpredictable, but certain factors bear on the scope of the "margin". A degree of European agreement or even harmonisation on an issue narrows that scope. If there is little or no agreement on the substantive issue, and no harmonisation of law, a state might be given a relatively wide margin of appreciation. Because societies are seen as differing substantially on the issue of what is "necessary" to protect "public morals" – they are allowed, for instance, to limit publications in their jurisdiction that are permitted elsewhere.

In practice the Court addresses freedom of expression only peripherally; it asks not whether the state in question struck the right balance between freedom of expression and competing interests, but rather whether the state restricted the right to such an extent that it brought itself outside the broad scope of what was more or less deemed to be acceptable throughout Europe. The only exception is when there are clear European standards in a specific field or when there is clear, strong convergence in European state practice.

For the purpose of this chapter, it suffices to note that the "margin of appreciation" continues to allow considerable differences in national standards on such things as pornography, incitement to racial hatred, defamation and privacy. As we shall discuss below, this poses serious problems in the new globalised digital environment.

Procedure and due process:
the ECHR and the international approach

The ECHR has two "due process" provisions. It requires:

- in Article 6, that states provide a "fair trial", with many specific guarantees, to anyone whose "civil rights and obligations" are "determined" in some forum, or faces a "criminal charge";
- in Article 13, that states provide an "effective remedy" to anyone whose ECHR rights and freedoms are violated.

In our opinion, any assessment of the legality and legitimacy of acts of political activism on the Internet ought to be determined in full and fair judicial proceedings fully conforming to the requirements of Article 6, ECHR.[236] That would bring European human rights law in line with the long-established principle expressed by the Supreme Court of the United States of America almost half a century ago that only a judicial determination in an adversary proceeding "suffices to impose a valid final restraint", because it "ensures the necessary sensitivity to freedom of expression".[237]

The Convention on Cybercrime:
weak reaffirmations of the basic principles

The Council of Europe Convention on Cybercrime, with its Additional Protocol, requires state parties to criminalise various activities in

---

236. Much case law, and academic debate on the Convention, has focused on the definition of "civil rights and obligations" and "criminal charge" – the qualifying factors for "fair trial" under Article 6 (if the issue is outside them, the person can rely only on the "effective remedy" of Article 13). We do not go into this distinction here, because in practice most cases related to political activism clearly fall within Article 6: they result from (criminal) investigation, prosecution, imprisonment or harassment; because the European Court of Human Rights increasingly reads elements of the judicial protection under Article 6 into the requirements of Article 13; and because we see the distinction as anachronistic – drafted in the 1950s when many states' due process in administrative (e.g. tax) law fell short of the "fair trial" requirements. Today, the ICCPR simply says that "everyone shall be entitled to a fair and public hearing by a competent, independent and impartial tribunal established by law" in determining any rights arising in any "suit at law" (criminal or not).
237. *Freedman v. Maryland*, 380 U.S. 51 (1965), available from: http://caselaw.lp. findlaw.com/scripts/getcase.pl?court=us&vol=380&invol=51.

cyberspace, including "distributing, or otherwise making available, racist and xenophobic material to the public through a computer system."

However, in our assessment its human rights provisions – covering process and procedure, substantive law, and interpretation – are generally weak, leaving the issues in question almost entirely to the states. In fact, they do little to clarify the ECHR requirements in cyberspace and should be strengthened through guidance and interpretation.

It is positive, however, that the convention contains provisions for the prohibition of indiscriminate surveillance and collection of large amounts of communications data.

The emerging Principles of Internet Governance

Certain principles stated by the Council of Europe Reykjavik Declaration and the Global Network Initiative (GNI) Principles, especially their emphasis on states' "positive obligations" and the responsibility of information and communication technology (ICT) companies (such as ISPs and search engines), make important contributions to ensuring effective respect for the human rights of online activists (and others). However, they do little to clarify how these high-minded principles should be applied in practice.

Two other documents go further, and spell out at least some further implications in some detail. These are Recommendation CM/Rec(2008)6 of the Council of Europe's Committee of Ministers on measures to promote respect for freedom of expression and information with regard to Internet filters, and the May 2011 Report of Frank La Rue, the UN Special Rapporteur on Freedom of Opinion and Expression, on the promotion and protection of the right to freedom of opinion and expression. Following on from the Rapporteur's previous (2010) report, the latter focuses on trends and challenges to all individuals' right to seek, receive and impart information and ideas of all kinds through the Internet.[238]

We shall discuss them in turn.

---

238. Human Rights Council, 17th session, 16 May 2011, A/HRC/17/27: www2.ohchr.org/english/bodies/hrcouncil/docs/17session/A.HRC.17.27_en.pdf.

The Reykjavik Declaration

In 2009 the Council of Europe Conference of Ministers responsible for Media and New Communication Services adopted the Reykjavik Declaration. The intention was to stress the need to ensure European human rights standards are upheld on the Internet. Though repeating commitments expressed, in similarly vague terms, in earlier declarations and recommendations,[239] the Reykjavik Declaration also notes the heavy reliance of the Internet on non-state actors (including private sector bodies such as ISPs), and on critical technical resources (such as "root servers" and "backbone structure") "which are controlled by a variety of government authorities, including re-designated defence agencies, academic institutions and private/business entities."[240]

The Reykjavik Declaration does not explicitly designate access to the Internet as a fundamental right, but comes close by stressing that "the notion of positive obligations developed in the case law of the European Court of Human Rights is particularly relevant in this context."[241] Also, the Committee of Ministers had already concluded in its recommendation on measures to promote the public service value of the Internet that "access to and the capacity and ability to use the Internet should be

---

239. See the long list and summaries of such earlier declarations and recommendations on p. 30 of the Background Text, at: www.coe.int/t/dghl/standardsetting/media-dataprotection/conf-internet-freedom/Internet%20governance_en.pdf.
240. Political declaration and resolutions from "A new notion of media ?" adopted by the Ministers responsible for Media and New Communication Services from the 1st Council of Europe Conference of Ministers responsible for Media and New Communication Services, held on 28 and 29 May 2009 in Reykjavik, available at: www.coe.int/t/dghl/standardsetting/media/MCM%282009%29011_en_final_web.pdf, in particular the Resolution on Internet governance and critical Internet resources (pp. 9-10) and the Resolution on developments in anti-terrorism legislation in Council of Europe member states and their impact on freedom of expression and information (pp. 11-12). These instruments include Resolution CM/Rec(2007)16, referred to later in the text.
241. Paragraph 3. See also paragraph 8: "Council of Europe member states share the responsibility to take reasonable measures to ensure the ongoing functioning of the Internet and, in consequence, of the delivery of the public service value to which all persons under their jurisdiction are entitled."

regarded as indispensable for the full exercise and enjoyment of human rights and fundamental freedoms in the information society.[242]

In other words, even if access to the Internet per se is not a human right, in the modern world all Council of Europe member states have a positive obligation to provide or at least a duty to allow it. Failure to do so, or measures to restrict access, inherently constitute interferences with rights protected under the ECHR, most notably the right to freedom to [seek,] receive and impart information and ideas regardless of frontiers, which is an integral part of the right to freedom of expression (Article 10, ECHR) and the right to respect for [confidentiality of one's] correspondence (an "autonomous concept" that has already been stretched to include all forms of communication) (Article 8, ECHR).[243]

The GNI Principles

The Principles on Freedom of Expression and Privacy drawn up by the GNI[244] make an important contribution by specifically including private sector entities in these obligations.

They include somewhat basic reaffirmations of the need for compliance on the Internet with international free expression and privacy standards, and even more basic references to the need for compliance

---

242. Recommendation CM/Rec(2007)16 of the Committee of Ministers on measures to promote the public service value of the Internet, at: https://wcd.coe.int/wcd/ViewDoc.jsp?id=1207291. See also the Internet Governance Principles, adopted at the COE conference "Internet freedom: From principles to global treaty law", April 2011, available in draft form at: www.coe.int/t/dghl/standardsetting/media-dataprotection/conf-internet-freedom/Internet%20Governance%20Principles.pdf.

243. This has been formally re-stated as the right to respect for one's communications in Article 7 of the EU Charter of Fundamental Rights.

244. GNI, founded in 2009, describes itself as "a diverse coalition of leading information and communications companies, major human rights organizations, academics, investors and technology leaders", who seek to protect and advance freedom of expression and privacy in ICTs. See: www.globalnetworkinitiative.org. This page also has links to the GNI Principles, the Implementation Guidelines for the Principles, and the Governance, Accountability and Learning Framework for the Principles.

with the rule of law in matters affecting freedom of expression on the Internet. But they add that ICT companies "have the responsibility to respect and protect the freedom of expression and privacy rights of their users" and that "the development of collaborative strategies involving business, industry associations, civil society organizations, investors and academics will be critical to the achievement of these principles." Subscribing companies must "integrate these principles into company decision making and culture through responsible policies, procedures and processes, and a transparent governance structure that supports their purpose and ensures their long-term success."

More specialised instruments and reports that add clarification and principles

In our opinion the Council of Europe Recommendation CM/Rec(2008)6 adds important new detail to the basic ECHR principles, in particular on transparency, procedural safeguards and involvement of the private sector. It sets out guidelines on use and application of broadly applied filters (that is, excluding user-controlled filters and those aimed at restricting access by children). These include protection for freedom of expression and privacy; requirements for filtering to be proportionate and only carried out by public bodies for reasons specified in Article 10.2 of the ECHR; and that blocking decisions be reviewable by an independent tribunal.

Report of the UN Special Rapporteur on Freedom of Opinion and Expression

The 2011 Report of the UN Special Rapporteur on Freedom of Opinion and Expression is a strong statement of the importance of freedom of expression and its exercise on the Internet.

The Rapporteur places great emphasis on the need for proper, judicial procedures in relation to anything that affects the right to Internet freedom of expression, contrasted with the arbitrariness he observes in many respects, including surveillance and monitoring of communications.

In terms of substantive law (what kinds of restriction on Internet free speech are warranted), he supports decriminalisation of defamation, worldwide. And on the important issue of censorship of alleged support for terrorism or terrorist organisations, he emphasises that national security or counter-terrorism measures can only be used to justify restricting the right to expression if the government can demonstrate that the expression is intended to incite imminent violence, is likely to incite such violence, and there is a direct and immediate connection between the expression and the likelihood or occurrence of such violence.

Quoting *Handyside* – that the right to freedom of expression includes "views and opinions that offend, shock or disturb" – and stating areas to which restrictions should never be applied (for example political debate; elections; reporting on human rights; government activities; corruption in government; peaceful demonstrations/political activities, including for peace or democracy; and expression of opinion, dissent, religion or belief, including by minorities/vulnerable groups), he emphasises the need for clear and unambiguous laws as a basis for any censorship/blocking/filtering, because broad, ambiguous laws are a basis for arbitrariness. He adds the important supplementary principle that:

> *Any legislation restricting the right to freedom of expression must be applied by a body which is independent of any political, commercial, or other unwarranted influences, in a manner that is neither arbitrary nor discriminatory, and with adequate safeguards against abuse, including the possibility of challenge and remedy against its abusive application.*

The Rapporteur says that blocking lists should not be secret, because "this makes it difficult to assess whether access is being restricted for a legitimate purpose", and that insufficiently targeted blocking measures that render a wide range of content inaccessible beyond that which has been deemed illegal are *ipso facto* an unnecessary or disproportionate means of achieving the purported aim.

He points out the drawbacks of "notice-and-takedown" measures, as "subject to abuse by both State and private actors", because intermediaries, as private entities, are not best placed to determine whether a particular content is illegal and "censorship measures should never be delegated to a private entity". He also notes that no one except the author should be held liable for content and that takedown should in principle occur only on a court order, after due process.

The Rapporteur welcomes the GNI, stressing that companies have duties, and that to avoid infringing users' rights to freedom of expression and privacy, intermediaries should: restrict these rights only after judicial intervention; be transparent to the user involved, and where applicable, to the wider public about measures taken; if possible forewarn users before taking restrictive measures; and minimise the impact of restrictions strictly to the content involved. Finally, there must be effective remedies for affected users, including appeal through procedures provided by the intermediary and by a competent judicial authority.

Problems in applying the emerging principles

The emerging body of principles indicates, more precisely than the basic principles of the ECHR or the case law under it, how the rights and freedoms (as well as duties and responsibilities) governing Internet political activism can, and cannot, be regulated. They centre on requirements for clearer laws reflecting strict substantive limits on limitations of free speech, applied by accountable bodies, and subject to judicial oversight; on shielding intermediaries from liability, subject to transparent *ex post facto* takedown procedures, again subject to effective judicial oversight; on imposition of duties on private sector entities (such as those intermediaries) to uphold freedom of expression, even where that conflicts with short-term commercial interests; and on guaranteeing unlimited access to the Internet for all.

We summarise these emerging principles in our conclusions and recommendations, and wholeheartedly endorse them. However, they do not resolve difficult legal issues under the relevant European and international standards, in particular the ECHR, which have been largely ignored or glossed over through vague statements merely reaffirming the need to uphold those standards. We believe this gives rise to a need to resolve three main difficulties in the:

- application of the "margin of appreciation" doctrine by the Strasbourg Court;
- rights and duties of private entities that play a crucial role in maintaining the Internet;
- guarantee of the rule of law and due process in everything related to the Internet.

The "margin of appreciation"

The doctrine of "the margin of appreciation" has resulted in uneven application of ECHR standards in different countries, even within the Council of Europe.

We believe the jurisdictional issue is central in relation to freedom of expression and communication, and thus to political activism, online. It can no longer be dismissed as a mere "difficulty" (as in the *Perrin* case, below): it is a core problem.

Under *Handyside*, courts in a European jurisdiction "A", could, today, order domestic ISPs to block content published from jurisdiction "B" (which could be a European or a non-European country) where its publication is legal, and could convict the author or publisher for breaching the domestic law of "A" (for instance for obscenity, incitement or defamation). The ban or conviction could be in accordance with the ECHR even if there were no ban anywhere else in Europe.

In the Strasbourg Court case with this profile – *Perrin v. the United Kingdom*[245] – a British court had convicted Perrin, a French national living in the UK, for a publication on a US-based site by a US-registered company he controlled. The UK Court asserted jurisdiction since the website could be accessed from the UK and the material was held to breach UK obscenity laws. However the site complied with its laws

---

245. Admissibility Decision of 18 October 2005 in Appl. No. 5446/03, *Perrin v. the United Kingdom*, accessed through HUDOC. The case is one of a number of cases listed in a May 2011 European Court of Human Rights Factsheet on new technologies, available at: www.echr.coe.int/NR/rdonlyres/CA9986C0-BF79-4E3D-9E36-DCCF1B622B62/0/FICHES_New_technologies_EN.pdf.

of origin (California, US). The issue was whether the material was obscene under Section 2 of the 1959 Obscene Publications Act. Perrin had argued that UK courts could convict only when the major steps towards publication took place in the UK;[246] the UK Court of Appeal ruled this would undermine the aim of the UK law, by encouraging publishers to take publication steps in countries where they were unlikely to be prosecuted, adding that "there is ... difficulty with the worldwide web, but it is through the worldwide web that people are able to make very substantial profits".

Nothing more was said about the "difficulty". Perrin submitted to the Court the argument on "major steps" in the UK being required for UK courts to have jurisdiction, but the Court dismissed it on the basis that as a UK resident, he had reasonable access to UK laws, and as the site was a professional activity, he could reasonably have been expected to be cautious in his occupation – and should have taken legal advice.

The Court referred to *Chauvy and Others v. France*, in which it had held that, as a professional, an applicant publisher must at least have been familiar with the applicable legislation and case law and could have sought advice from specialist counsel. But this was for a hard-copy, offline publication, in France, by French applicants, with no international aspect.

We feel that in *Perrin* the Strasbourg Court did not sufficiently address the crucial issue, and accepted applicability of UK law too readily, without sufficiently detailed reasoning. By simply dismissing the jurisdictional point, it missed an opportunity to clarify application of the ECHR to Internet publication. It failed to seriously examine the closeness or otherwise of the link between the applicant, the US company, and the UK, for example in terms of visitors to the website.

In the *Yahoo!* case, a French court ordered Yahoo! of the US to block access to US-based auctions of Nazi items or content denying the

---

246. Here we are not discussing whether the Obscene Publications Act is clear enough to be regarded as "law" in terms of the ECHR, nor whether the applicants' conviction was disproportionate, for example.

Holocaust. Yahoo! argued that such an order could not apply in the US, as it would violate the US Constitution's First Amendment (guaranteeing freedom of speech to every citizen). But the order was imposed. The case has not been taken to the Strasbourg Court; the US courts have refused to deal with the issues of principle.[247]

In an academic note a decade ago,[248] Tim Fitzpatrick noted that if a German judgment can rule any website accessible from Germany to be subject to German law, websites would be subject to the laws of every country, resulting in an anarchic legal framework fraught with contradictions. The *Yahoo!* case foreshadowed the challenge of creating a global governance system: that of determining when a foreign court can make a valid, binding ruling over an Internet company. If the process gathered momentum, he said, "the legal infrastructure that the Internet is built upon" would "crumble under the weight of unlimited and unsolvable conflict"; while on the other hand, if countries cannot regulate, many countries' fragile social compromises might be undermined.

The dilemma remains unresolved. Guidance is urgently required. It could come from the Strasbourg Court, intergovernmental guidelines or a treaty.

---

247. See the Case Analysis of the International League Against Racism and Anti-semitism (LICRA), *French Union of Jewish Students v. Yahoo! Inc.* (USA), Yahoo France, Tribunal de Grande Instance de Paris (The County Court of Paris), Interim Court Order, 20 November, 2000, by Yaman Akdeniz, at: www.cyber-rights.org/documents/yahoo_ya.pdf. As this case summary notes: "The French approach ... is similar to the German approach in which Compuserve was found liable under German criminal law for the distribution of illegal content over the Internet (mainly child pornography). The [German] decision came despite the efforts of the Prosecution who agreed with the defence that 'it was technically impossible to filter out all such material' over the Internet." Local court (Amtsgericht) Munich, English version of the case at: www.cyber-rights.org/isps/somm-dec.htm. See also "[U.S.] Court throws out Yahoo appeal in Nazi memorabilia case", 12 January 2006, by Juan Carlos Perez, at www.infoworld.com/print/20138.

248. Fitzpatrick T. "Establishing personal jurisdiction in cyberspace: Can anyone govern Yahoo?", UCLA J.L. & Tech. Notes 1, at: www.lawtechjournal.com/notes/2001/01_010417_fitzpatrick.php.

In view of the crucial need to preserve the Internet's openness, neutrality and limited regulation (principles strongly supported by the Council of Europe),[249] we feel the Strasbourg Court's current approach is too accommodating to member states and cannot be retained without modification in the context of the Internet; it leads inevitably to those "unlimited and unsolvable conflict[s]". Member states should no longer be given the excessive protection of overgenerous application of the "margin of appreciation" on the Internet.

Solutions are not easy; but neither member states nor the Strasbourg Court should chase chimeras. The pretence that member states can stop the sea of information at their virtual borders by court order is unsustainable.

Ordering intermediaries to filter out search results, or ISPs to block transmission of an e-book, does not prevent access to it by anyone keen to find it; such measures are trivially easy to circumvent – while their imposition signals that states remain free to impose their own divergent restrictions.

Overcoming Yahoo!

There is an important distinction to be made between material that is unlawful in one country but not in others, and material that is unlawful under international law. In our opinion, in cases where material is legal to produce and disseminate in one country, and illegal in others, the law should be directed at those who download the material. The state that has criminalised this material ought to focus on its own jurisdiction and prosecute those who download. If instead the law is directed at intermediaries, such as ISPs, it will be largely ineffective in tackling both the production and availability of the material and will have a significant detrimental effect on free expression.

We believe Perrin's conviction could be compatible with the ECHR if it was shown that he had personal primary responsibility for the

---

249. See in particular the Council of Europe's draft Internet Governance Principles and CM/Rec(2007)6.

materials: that the site specifically targeted or clearly attracted UK visitors in significant numbers – and that no measures were in place to dissuade UK visitors from entering the site.

Those who oppose certain content may not be satisfied with our proposal, but should understand that convictions such as Perrin's and blocking orders like that against Yahoo! are of limited effectiveness in preventing access to the material. We consider such measures to be neither necessary nor proportionate. Also, if Perrin's conviction was to stop him "corrupting morals", it may stop him while in prison, but will not prevent seekers finding comparable sites publishing from anywhere, nor imitators.

In the case of material that is unlawful under international law (child abuse images, incitement to racial hatred, etc.), states should take action to prohibit materials, here primarily targeting producers rather than consumers. States should take steps to co-operate in doing so.

For all material that is unlawful in one country, but not others, we suggest it must be established whether a restriction is compatible with substantive European and international standards; then it must be determined whether it obeys the requirement of the UN Special Rapporteur and the UN Human Rights Council, that restrictions should never be applied to political debate, reporting on human rights, government activities or corruption, election campaigns, peaceful demonstrations or political activities, or expression of opinion, dissent, religion or belief.

This would leave states the right to impose restrictions on certain forms of material such as pornography or incitement. But, on these, states should no longer be given wide margins of appreciation as to freedom of expression. They should be allowed to impose measures on their own nationals and residents, for downloading materials that are unlawful under their domestic law (provided that the domestic law complies with the ECHR). But they should not be allowed to penalise companies and individuals in other countries where the materials are lawful (and not contrary to international criminal law), for making the materials available.

Rights and duties of private sector entities

The ECHR governs action (or inaction) by states, not private entities. States' duties are mainly "negative", for example to abstain from torture. But in some cases the Strasbourg Court has imposed "positive obligations" on states – including to "secure" enjoyment of a right.[250] When it extends these to matters between private parties, this is called the ECHR's "indirect horizontal effect": it has held, for example, that a state has a duty to stop employers from dismissing people who refuse to accept compulsory trade union membership,[251] and to provide sanctions against a man who abused a child with intellectual disability.[252] Impositions causing these indirect effects are rare, and the ruling is against the state, not the private transgressor. It is left to the state to decide how to deal with the private entity – and the state is left a very wide margin of appreciation to choose measures to ensure respect for the relevant right.

We believe that securing rights to communication, expression and association on the Internet, vis-à-vis ISPs, search engines and blog hosts, for instance, should not be left to the very indirect, haphazard application of "horizontal effect".

The emerging Internet governance principles, including the GNI Principles on Freedom of Expression and Privacy, have recognised this. We believe these (or similar) principles should be given greater legal backing as a vital precondition for protection of human rights in the information society.

One way of achieving this would be through the conditioning of the invocability of intermediary (especially ISP) liability exceptions upon compliance with such a self-regulatory initiative. This means that as

---

250. See the requirement in Article 1 of the ECHR that all state parties "shall secure to everyone within their jurisdiction the rights and freedoms defined in Section I of this Convention."
251. *Young, James and Webster v. the United Kingdom*, Appl. Nos. 7601/76, 7806/77, judgment of 18 October 1982.
252. *X and Y v. the Netherlands*. Appl. No. 8978/80, judgment of 26 March 1985.

long as the intermediary (ISP) follows certain rules and procedures (as set out in such initiatives), it will not be liable for any act by its customers alleged to be in breach of criminal or civil law. See, for example, Articles 12 to 15 of the EU E-Commerce Directive,[253] or s.230 of the US Communications Decency Act.[254]

The substantive and procedural rules in question could be endorsed (formally or otherwise) in national or European law. This is a new area, and new, "blue-sky" thinking is needed. However, we note that one alternative, the creation of yet more treaty systems, is not much encouraged these days.

With significant endorsement, such a system of rules might be a major means to ensure good governance, and respect for fundamental rights, on the Internet, especially if it included a reporting and supervisory mechanism (now usual in international human rights treaties). It might gain added force if companies that signed up to it would obtain some benefit (other than goodwill), such as allowing states to give them preferential treatment in the awarding of Internet-related contracts, without being in breach of World Trade Organization rules.

The rule of law and due process: guaranteeing compliance

We have deliberately emphasised the less difficult, but crucial (and not yet resolved) issue of the rule of law and due process. Our points are in line with similar views of the UN Rapporteur. We recommend that:

–   any interference with the freedoms to communicate, express views or organise be based on rules that are clear, specific and accessible. Given these freedoms' crucial importance, such rules should to a very large extent be spelled out in statute law (rather than left to subsidiary rules or ministerial orders, for example, which can be too easily made and quickly changed, and are often insufficiently accessible);

---

253. Directive 2000/31/EC of the European Parliament and of the Council, 8 June 2000, on legal aspects of information society services, in particular e-commerce, in the Internal Market ("Directive on electronic commerce"), OJ L 178, 17.7.2000, p. 1-16.
254. 47 USC para. 230.

- these rules prevent arbitrariness: any authority to which the power to apply them is delegated should not be given excessive discretion, should be required to give reasoned rulings, and should be subject to judicial supervision:
  - substantive restrictions on freedom of expression should obey the limitations on such restrictions spelled out by the UN Special Rapporteur on Freedom of Opinion and Expression and the UN Human Rights Council (as quoted above);
  - any surveillance measures must respect the prohibition (in the Convention on Cybercrime) on "general or indiscriminate surveillance and collection of large amounts of traffic [and communications] data". Compulsory suspicionless retention of such data, currently required under EU law, violates this principle and also, in our view, the ECHR and the EU Charter, as well as several national constitutions;
- any blocking or filtering be based on published lists or criteria, drawn up by properly designated bodies, supervised and accountable under public law or to parliament;
- actual blocking be in principle carried out only after due notice to those involved (both the owners of sites to be blocked and the public), since blocking a site not only prevents the host from publishing, but everyone else from receiving;
- such notice be followed by proper, full, public judicial proceedings (in very urgent cases, a judge should be able to issue temporary injunctions, on the usual restricted basis and subject to equally urgent hearings and challenges);
- legal aid be available to those affected, including civil society groups with an interest in the case, who should be given right of standing, for instance through class actions: individuals and civil society groups should not have to face punitive financial risks for taking such action;
- to the extent that entities of the private sector impose or give effect to restrictions on the above freedoms, they be subject to the above conditions exactly in the same way as entities of the public

sector, possibly through the new international rules discussed above, and pending that, by their state of establishment taking responsibility for their actions, and through enforceable "third party beneficiary" clauses in relevant contracts, etc.

Conclusions and recommendations

We have examined the significant human rights issues raised for member states of the Council of Europe by the potential of online social media as a tool of political activism, as recently demonstrated by events in the Middle East and North Africa, and state counter-measures they have provoked: in particular, Internet blocking, takedown procedures and Internet surveillance (including surveillance-facilitating measures such as compulsory data retention).

These measures have become increasingly prevalent in Council of Europe member states due to legitimate state concerns about online criminal activities, particularly online exchange of child abuse images. However, due to the limitations inherent in these restrictive measures, Internet blocking does not serve the aim of removing targeted content from the Internet (and does little, for example, to protect children from abuse). It is highly intrusive; ineffective in preventing determined users from accessing illegal content; inevitably blocks legal content; and can sometimes assist those against whom it is used.

Moreover, it is often based on vague, arbitrary laws (or no law at all); usually relies on secret lists, unknown to the public and drawn up by unaccountable bodies; and is seriously lacking in due process, both when applied as prevention – with exclusion of stakeholders, notification and a right to object to blocking – and after the fact, in terms of challengeability (would-be publishers and recipients are both unable effectively to challenge lists or decisions).

Far from providing a free, unwatched space for social and political interaction, Internet technologies can facilitate potentially comprehensive surveillance over online political action – increasingly linked to offline surveillance of political activities, in particular through "social network analysis" and "profiling". This is facilitated in a most pernicious way, not only in manifestly repressive countries but also in modern democracies through compulsory suspicionless mass communication data retention under the EU's Data Retention Directive. Such measures have been held to violate fundamental rights and basic principles of the rule of law by national constitutional courts in several EU member states, and by the European Data Protection Supervisor.

The Strasbourg Court has established basic principles relating to the closely linked rights of communication, expression and association. Restrictions on these freedoms must be based on legal rules that meet important "quality" requirements of clarity, accessibility and foreseeability; that serve a "pressing social need"; are "necessary" to achieve that purpose, implying that they shall not be disproportionate or ineffective; and offer an "effective remedy", preferably judicial, against such restrictions.

The Council of Europe's Convention on Cybercrime contains rather basic, and qualified, affirmations of these principles, but also a more useful prohibition against "general or indiscriminate surveillance and collection of large amounts of traffic [and communications] data".

Emerging principles of Internet governance reflect a growing consensus on the need for principles governing the activities of private sector entities involved in the maintenance of the Internet, or as intermediaries between the Internet and individual users. There have also recently been important new clarifications and developments of the well-established principles in relation to the Internet, as contained in particular in Council of Europe Committee of Ministers Recommendation CM/Rec(2008)6 and especially the May 2011 Report of the UN Special Rapporteur on Freedom of Opinion and Expression to the UN Human Rights Council.

There are a number of difficulties in applying these new, emerging principles relating to online freedoms of communication, expression and association. We have identified three issues that cause particular problems in this regard.

First, in an age of global communication and information exchanges, states should no longer be given the excessive protection accorded to them by the overgenerous application of the "margin of appreciation" doctrine. We propose a much more restrictive application of the doctrine, to deal with the reality of the Internet, because in our opinion the pretence that states can stop the sea of information at their virtual borders is unsustainable.

Second, we conclude that the ECHR as currently applied is insufficient to regulate the actions of private entities involved in the day-to-day operation of the Internet. It should not be left to the indirect, haphazard application of the doctrine of horizontal effect to secure the rights to communication, expression and association of everyone, including political activists, on the Internet vis-à-vis ISPs, search engines and blog hosts, for example.

In our opinion, the emerging Internet governance principles (which specifically extend to private sector entities) should become legally enforceable. This could be achieved through minor, but crucial, changes to existing rules on intermediary liability.

Finally, we have spelled out in some detail the requirements of the rule of law, as we see them, in relation to political activity on the Internet. These include:

- the need to base all restrictions on clear, specific and accessible rules, in statute law;
- limits on delegated authority and on measures that could lead to arbitrariness;
- transparency over Internet blocking;
- the establishment of due process and *ex post facto* judicial procedures in respect of blocking, with full involvement of civil society.

The private sector entities that effectively control much of what happens on the Internet must also play a key role in protecting these principles.

We believe that the adoption of the above recommendations would greatly strengthen the legal protection of online political activism, and ensure that the potential of the Internet to support human rights is fully developed.

Freedom of expression on the Internet is a fundamental freedom of our age. Together with Internet privacy, it is vital to our freedoms to communicate and associate, and to collectively determine how our societies should be run.

Acronyms and terms

Blocking – to prevent specific content from reaching a final user (child abuse images, for example)

CoE – Council of Europe

The Court – European Court of Human Rights

Data retention – the storage of client communication records by communication service providers (including ISPs)

Data Retention Directive – requires EU member states to compel providers of e-communication services to store traffic and location data of the communications of all citizens for possible use by member states for law enforcement

ECHR – European Convention on Human Rights

EDRi – European Digital Rights – a group containing different organisations that have joined forces to defend civil rights in the information society

External pluralism – pluralism across multiple outlets

Filtering – see "Blocking"

GNI – Global Network Initiative – a non-governmental organisation working with Internet access issues and Internet privacy rights

ICT – Information and Communication Technology

ICCPR – International Covenant on Civil and Political Rights, UN General Assembly Resolution 2200A (XXI), (1966)

ICESCR – International Covenant on Economic, Social and Cultural Rights, UN General Assembly Resolution 2200A (XXI), (1966)

Internal pluralism – pluralism within a single medium

Internet surveillance – gathering of information about who communicates with whom – including measures that facilitate this, such as compulsory data retention

ISP – Internet service provider

OWNI – a media innovation group

OSCE – Organization for Security and Co-operation in Europe

OSI – Open Society Institute

PACE – Parliamentary Assembly of the Council of Europe

PCC – Press Complaints Commission – an independent self-regulatory body in the UK which deals with complaints about the editorial content of newspapers and magazines (and their websites)

PSM – public service media – media that produce and transmit public interest content. PSM has a wider scope in terms of services than PSB, because it includes both traditional media and new media

PSB – public service broadcasting

SNS – social networking site

The Strasbourg Court – European Court of Human Rights

UDHR – Universal Declaration of Human Rights (1948)